This book arrived as a gift

It is given as a gift

Spread Kindness, share books

@wanderingbookseller

being relaxes, and a tear comes as a sign of relief. This book is a new kind of church that genuinely gives *all* of us the refuge we need."

—**Sah D'Simone**, author of *Spiritually Sassy*
and *5-Minute Daily Meditations*

"What a gift this book is. Kevin put all the wonderful aspects of an intimate conversation with them in this helpful resource."

—**Scott Erickson**, author of *Honest Advent* and *Say Yes*

"For a world of us budded humans seeking a space to bloom intentionally, purposely, and freely into our divine and connected selves, Garcia offers not a guide but a single stone on a path we have been conditioned to believe that we can't create ourselves. Every meditation, reflective exercise, and gentle offering allows our learned petals of shame and guilt to unfold into freedom and safety. *What Makes You Bloom* is the sunshine we wanderers need to find the light and learn what it means to find it for ourselves time and time again."

—**Arielle Estoria**, actor, poet, and author of *The Unfolding:
An Invitation to Come Home to Yourself*

"For my fellow exvangelical wanderers looking for a way forward: this book is for you. Regardless of where you come from or where you're going, Garcia's *What Makes You Bloom* puts the practical in spiritual practice, giving you real tools to find your own path of becoming."

—**Brandon Flanery**, journalist, digital creator, and author of
Stumbling: A Sassy Memoir about Coming Out of Evangelicalism

"Kevin Garcia finds their voice in *What Makes You Bloom*. It's a guide for anyone whose spiritual search ended when they left the church building—for good reasons. Garcia's writing is captivating and deeply insightful, inspiring readers to pursue their passions and live a life that truly makes them bloom. I highly recommend this gem of a book to all the spiritual questers out there who are looking to ignite their inner spark and find their place in the world."

—**Tripp Fuller**, host of the *Homebrewed Christianity* podcast and visiting professor of theology at Luther Seminary

"A life truly lived is one that bravely traverses both the chill of winter and the vibrant renewal of spring. It knows that in order to grow, it must shed its old leaves and patiently rest before wildly blooming once more. Kevin, with their compassionate heart and courageous spirit, serves as a gentle reminder of the resilience and bravery needed to flourish in this wild and magnificent journey we call life."

—**Julianna Glasse**, inspirational speaker, author, and host of the Read With Jules book club

"Kevin Miguel Garcia found a way to meet the reader where they are at in their journey, express tough love to help them through the process of discovering new ways of thinking, and offer guidance throughout. Their personal stories and experiences constantly affirm for the reader that they aren't alone and that growth and evolution are always possible. Anyone at any place in their spiritual journey will find comfort, healing, and hope in this book."

—**Malynda Hale**, singer/actress, activist, and host of *#WeNeedToTalk* podcast

"I've often said that you get to decide how to be spiritual. Kevin Garcia's new book furnishes the 'how' beautifully. Kevin weaves personal experiences, stories, and ideas throughout a book full of simple practices to enhance our personal spiritual lives in healthy, courageous, and beneficial ways. I would also consider it a practical manual for recovery from religious trauma. If you're saying 'I'm deconstructing. Now what?'—read this book."

—**David Hayward**, artist known as @NakedPastor
and author of *Flip It Like This!*

"Kevin Garcia's voice is one of beautiful disruption: honest, sincere, and vibrant. Their undeniable love for the community and how our oneness is deeply connected to a more fluid and open divinity continues to create more space and liberation for queer-identifying and non-queer folks alike."

—**Joél Leon**, author and storyteller

"The perfect example of integration, *What Makes You Bloom* is a seamless blend of ancient wisdom with modern insight, irreverence woven into an accessible and nourishing sacred lens on all things, and truth-telling that is at once gentle and incisive. This book is sure to wake you up, stretch you, and affirm you."

—**Hillary McBride**, PhD, registered psychologist, podcaster,
speaker, and author of *The Wisdom of Your Body*

"*What Makes You Bloom* is a delicious combination of the practices my friend Kevin Garcia used to aid in their spiritual recovery and the practical wisdom gleaned from the well-worn path they've journeyed with clients and community members. In this book, you'll go beyond cheap religion to build a life of beauty and meaning. If you want to come alive, from the depths of your soul radiating outward, this book is for you."

—**Brian G. Murphy**, co-founder of QueerTheology.com
and owner of Relationshift

"*What Makes You Bloom* offers a beautiful vision of a liberated spirituality. It is a vital exploration of what it means to be human, where Garcia encourages us to embrace all the complexities that reside within ourselves. This is not a book that offers up easy answers; instead, it asks vital questions about our minds, our bodies, our communities, and the ways we can better care for one another. Every chapter in this book is imbued with a deep sense of hope, beauty, and most importantly, love."

—**Jonathan Parks-Ramage**, author of *Yes, Daddy: A Novel*

"This book is a start. Usually when people say something is 'a start,' they mean it in a bad way, as if there is something lacking. That's not how I mean it. There is no lack here. But *What Makes You Bloom* won't make your life better just by reading it. Instead, Kevin shows us how to begin. They show us how to start to shake free from what has kept us bound, and how to keep going when things get hard. It is a start, and if you're looking for a new start, this book will be a welcome guide."

—**Matthias Roberts**, psychotherapist and author of *Holy Runaways* and *Beyond Shame*

"Kevin Miguel Garcia is a natural-born truth-teller! And in *What Makes You Bloom*, their storytelling, vulnerability, passions, and voice all come together to deliver truth, sometimes an uncomfortable truth, with earnest delight. Garcia's words are wise, winsome, and potent, a powerful offering to help all of us blossom into our truest selves."

—**Matthew Paul Turner**, #1 *New York Times*–bestselling author of *What Is God Like?*

"If you've ever had that niggling feeling that God is far more abundant and generous than what you were taught as a kid and there's nothing wrong with how you arrived in this world, Kevin Miguel Garcia's *What Makes You Bloom* is here to help you to be radically honest and 'tell the truth all the time about everything [that is every part of you] to everyone.'"

—**Marcie Alvis Walker**, creator of the *Black Coffee with White Friends* website and author of *Everybody Come Alive*

"We are only just beginning to comprehend how powerful love is, how much it asks of the ego to rescind, how much it asks of the soul to rise. We are only just beginning to comprehend how much of Christ's teachings are about seeing ourselves and others with love—a love that liberates. One part memoir, one part manifesto for healing from Christianity, and one part workbook for putting a love that liberates into practice, Kevin Garcia's *What Makes You Bloom* offers us the chance to live in radical alignment with the truth of who we are—and there's nothing more divine than that."

—**Meggan Watterson**, MDiv, MTS, *Wall Street Journal* bestselling author of *Mary Magdalene Revealed*

What Makes You Bloom

WHAT MAKES
YOU BLOOM

Cultivating a Practice for
Connecting with Your Divine Self

KEVIN MIGUEL GARCIA

Broadleaf Books
Minneapolis

WHAT MAKES YOU BLOOM
Cultivating a Practice for Connecting with Your Divine Self

Library of Congress Cataloging-in-Publication Data

Names: Garcia, Kevin Miguel, author.
Title: What makes you bloom : cultivating a practice for connecting with your divine self / Kevin Miguel Garcia.
Description: Minneapolis : Broadleaf Books, [2024]
Identifiers: LCCN 2023009967 (print) | LCCN 2023009968 (ebook) | ISBN 9781506493589 (print) | ISBN 9781506493596 (ebook)
Subjects: LCSH: Self-actualization (Psychology)--Religious aspects. | Meditation. | Spiritual life.
Classification: LCC BV4598.2 .G37 2024 (print) | LCC BV4598.2 (ebook) | DDC 158.1--dc23/eng/20230614
LC record available at https://lccn.loc.gov/2023009967
LC ebook record available at https://lccn.loc.gov/2023009968

Cover design: Gabe Nansen

Print ISBN: 978-1-5064-9358-9
eBook ISBN: 978-1-5064-9359-6

Printed in China.

To every person who has lost something when they started asking questions. You're not alone, and you are never forgotten. This offering is for you. You are welcome at this crowded table.

CONTENTS

CONTENTS

FOREWORD

It's lovely that Kevin has asked me to write the foreword for their beautiful book. We are friendly, not close, but vibe on each other, love each other. We see something in each other, some kind of mirrored image. They're brilliant; I like to think I am too. They are funny; ask my friends—they'll tell you that I think I am hilarious. Kevin has a deep reservoir of wisdom hewn in their own suffering at the hands of church, church folk, and toxic religion. Wisdom fertilized with their humor and determination to bloom where they stand.

Kevin stands on the edge of the faith we both inherited from our people, the one we both rejected, the one we know scarred us and others like us. We've both walked away from that edgy place, deciding, instead, to center flourishing, love, grace, authentic joy. We both know the toxicity will kill us, kill all of us, will wound our souls with deep scars that bleed out the Life Source until we wither up and die. And we are both determined not to die, but to live.

As I write, I hear the epilogue in *Les Misérables*, Jean Valjean's final poignant prayer, "let me be . . . take me now . . . take me home." Cosette's return, offering forgiveness, fiercely loving the man who raised her, loving him—willing him—to life, even as he dies. "You will live, Papa, you're going to live, it's too soon, too soon to say goodbye." The love, the grace, the forgiveness, offering the stuff that blooms us to life. If there is a resurrection, it is love that makes us live forever. If there is such a thing as salvation, it is love that saves us. If there is a God, it is loving one another that makes that God visible.

Take my hand and lead me to salvation, take my love for love is ever-lasting and remember the truth that once was spoken to love another person is to see the face of God.

I believe this is the hymn of Kevin's religion, sung in the key of the truth that makes them bloom, makes me bloom. Love is the aim—love that is gentle on us, love gentle toward our people, love gentle even toward the stranger. Love fierce enough to be kind, to offer fresh starts, love that can say, "Nope, I'm not going to make that deadline, hit that mark, earn that reward; I'm not going to be perfect today. I'm going to be. Perfectly me, where I am, as I am. I am going to bloom here."

And the people sing, walk behind the plowshare, put away the sword. Put away the swords that cut our hearts out. Put away the sharp judgements, the pointed blaming, the double-edged theologies that impinge and crush our souls. Put away the soul-crushing, deadening, suffocating, crucifying patterns in which we live as though we are dead-people-walking. Punishing schedules that drive us madly on repeat, competitive capitalism that makes us think we are living when we are simply existing.

In one of my favorite TikToks this year, Kevin is loving themself to bloom. "My book manuscript was due yesterday. Is it done? No. I'm gonna work my tail off, but I know it's gonna be a little late. And I am so ok with that. . . . I'm very ambitious and sometimes I overpromise things. But maybe I should cut myself some slack. Maybe I should underestimate myself a little more. But what's different about this time versus all the other times that I've been late on something, or that I haven't met a deadline or a goal: I'm not beating myself up over this. I'm not calling myself a bad person or lazy. I'm just okay. And now I'm going to go work on it. So give yourself some love today, you're doing the best you can."

Doing the best you can. That's what makes us bloom. Kevin's words sing my life. They will sing yours, too.

—The Rev. Dr. Jacqui Lewis, Senior Minister and Public Theologian at Middle Church in Manhattan, where love blooms. She is the author of *Fierce Love: A Bold Path to Ferocious Courage and Rule Breaking Kindness That Can Heal the World.*

READ THIS FIRST

An Introduction to What Makes You Bloom

I'm making some inferences about you, the person who picked up this book and is reading it. I'm assuming you've got some Christian faith background. Whether or not you call yourself a Christian now doesn't concern me to be honest. I just want you to be honest with yourself. I'm also assuming that you maybe have some beef with the church, or at least misgivings. You grew up in it, or you converted later in life. Either way, you probably wholeheartedly believed. Or at least you wanted to. And you tried really, really hard for a really, really long time to say with all the conviction you could muster that you believed as everyone around you did.

Until you didn't.

And then things probably got dicey. Your friends from church began asking you to get coffee, maybe alongside the pastor to ask, "How's your walk with Jesus?" You searched for the words to describe how you and Jesus were on a break because you were concerned about the church's behavior issues. You talked about your experiences, how your gay friend was more loving than that one asshole on the committee you serve on at church. You recounted how your Muslim friend invited you to break fast with

1

their family after Ramadan. You wondered if a loving God could send people to eternal, conscious torment and still be loving.

And even after telling them how this new way of thinking, this new way of believing felt more true, how it might be drawing you closer to God even, their concern boiled over. And when you told them there is no need to be concerned, they fired off.

You never really believed.
You're doing this for the attention.
You've got an unspoken sin you don't want to give up.
You're being deceived by the devil.
You just haven't really met Jesus yet.
You're abandoning God.
You're abandoning the church.
You're abandoning us.
You you you you you.
It's always you. It's your fault this is happening.

And eventually, you couldn't take it anymore because these fucking people would not listen to you. People you have loved and respected forever, some who you swore fidelity unto death to, suddenly attached terms and conditions to their love, withdrawing their respect and offering punishment instead. And you left. Either silently or loudly. Regardless, there is a pang in your chest when you realize how the church will erase you from community memory. There is a feeling of anger brewing inside when you consider all the shit they are going to talk about you. But still, you would never go back. You could never go back.

And here you are, reading this and possibly wondering if there is something beyond the pain of letting go of something and of a bunch of someones you really loved. You are wondering if there's still a place for you in the family of God, or maybe you're just wondering what your home is in this vast universe, on this planet with this beloved family of things we call the physical world.

I'm happy to say yes. There is something beyond heartache. There is something beyond loss. There is something beyond the small conceptions, the limited perceptions of Love that we have placed upon it. There is something beyond a shallow understanding of ancient holy books and beyond the emotional highs created by smoke screens, lights, and cinematic-level music. There is more. So much more. And the best part?

You don't have to go anywhere, do anything, or be anybody special to experience it.

My love, I want to tell you about how I found Peace. And I say Peace with a capital P because it is God to me, the same way I say Love with a capital L. The sweet, delicious, unwavering presence of Peace is always available to us. It is merely our awareness that is impaired. Only our perceptions limit our ability to see and feel Love, to experience Peace, Here and Now.

Let me give you some of my story:

I've been deconstructing my faith since before it was cool. Before the term was used in relation to Christian faith, before TikTok evangelists for both sides stitched each other's content for supremacy. Before pastors took any of what we were saying seriously. We've come a long way in the last decade. And to be frank, a long way looks like a spiritual refugee camp outside the empire's walls. One way I heard Nadia Bolz-Weber put it in a podcast episode we did together: out here in the wild unknown, past our normal spaces, it feels like we're on the same team, but we only score points if we are shitty to each other. We still try to out-holy each other. I see people get into fights online, looking for an enemy still lurking in anyone and anything that looks like it could be their trauma returning. Capitalism, patriarchy, and empire have us turning on one another instead of turning inward. Our bodies are traumatized, and our minds can scarcely find Peace.

I went on a big-ass mission trip after college. Eleven months to eleven countries (I only made it seven of those months) with forty-nine of the most purity cultured, indoctrinated, emotionally damaged, codependent, sold-out Christians I've ever met. We bopped around the world. When times got hard, man, did our trauma show itself off! It was a huge mess, and we all knew it. Some of us smiled and towed the party line, ignoring bad behavior, ignoring our legit complaints. We barely knew how to be kind to one another, let alone take responsibility for our care. We were loyally and stupidly following an organization of leaders who didn't care about the impact, just that they facilitated this trip. They didn't care about our mental health. Hell, they didn't care about our health, period. Then there were those of us that realized that this was bad. This wasn't good for us, for our minds and souls. If I wanted to make it out alive, and I mean that literally, I had to leave. That was the first stop in my spiritual desert. Pretty soon after I got home though, my evangelical subconscious mind training kicked in.

I felt guilty for how I left. Even though I was a danger to myself, even though I forked over the dollars to get me home so I could get some stability (i.e., save my own life), even though I was my hero, I condemned myself for not being better and for not being more faithful. And that guilt drove me back to work for this organization in an "apprenticeship program," which was one of those "internships" where you pay to work for them through support raising. And again, it was for the kingdom! So why not.

Fast forward just six months, to the summer of 2015, I cracked under the pressure of trying to be a good boyfriend to a wonderful Christian woman with phenomenal taste in home decor. I came out, and every single one of my leaders got a message from the Holy Spirit that it was not my time to continue at this organization. Funny how that works, eh? I wound up living with my friend Casey, sharing a room in the basement because I was even more broke and in debt after giving my free labor to this group who called me family. I again found myself mad at God for leading me into a place of nothingness. I did all this for You. I did all You asked me, and this? This is what I get?

Yes.
This is what you get, Kevin.
You left that place.
You are here now.
And you *asked* for this, Kevin.

Isn't that interesting?

We don't often realize that we've got that much power. We don't realize the spiritual wildernesses, the liminal spaces, the discomfort—all of it is something we asked for. Maybe not even knowingly, but I believe that deep down, every soul wants to know the truth. Every soul seeks its reflection in this physical world. And for a while, we find that reflection in the systems we were born into. We learn to be good little Christian kids and grow up to be good Christian men and women, and if the hegemony surrounds you with American Christianity, you have no reason to question it.

Until you do.

There are days I miss my old community. However, I could not go back to work or even volunteer with that old organization. I couldn't dream of shrinking myself to fit into their definition of faithful. Even when I was stuck living in that shit-ass basement apartment that I shared with another fully grown-ass man, even during that struggle was better than lying to myself and others to get their approval. I'd rather endlessly struggle to be who I am than easily lie about who I'm not.

I no longer blamed myself when I realized I got myself here. I realized I was the one who rescued me. My conditioning and trauma wanted to tell me that I was unfaithful and God was punishing me, but I was faithful to God. I was devoted to my calling to be my most authentic self—our only calling ever. I was convinced my worth aligned with my bank account, what ministry I was doing, and what I could create that was helpful to others. If only I were working harder, I would feel better. That is capitalism, baby! That is a lie. And it's a lie I still catch myself believing and operating from.

Leaving a religious space that doesn't help you flourish is the pursuit of God. No matter what they tell you.

I got myself here. I got myself out of that place that was killing me. That's so powerful. This discomfort? It's expected. I knew it would hurt to let go. This fear of the unknown? I had that when I was still in the middle of Churchland. At least now I'm not ignoring it. So, I could complain that I don't have those connections anymore or realize that I don't actually want those connections or relationships anymore. This led me to a new question:

What do I want?

What do I want to feel and do and be on the other side of all this shit?

On the other side of the questions, many of which I know are unanswerable, what would be nice?

I wanted to feel safe and at ease. I wanted to feel held by a (likely) benevolent universe. I wanted to do things that made me happy with people who made me happy. I just wanted to be okay. That would be nice.

That first year out of the closet grew me up quickly. I feel like I went through my childhood, teens, and twenties all at once. Contrary to what my pastors told me, I feel like I am closer to whatever or whoever God is than I was when I was trying to be a straight worship artist who was merely desperate to be loved. This feeling of Peace, this feeling of continuous Joy, this overflowing Kindness, the sense of connectedness to everyone and everything, none of it is an accident.

None of this is magic. It's math.

Said another way: it's all cause and effect. If you do a thing, something will happen. When you keep up a habit, something changes. It is no different with your thoughts and emotions. It is no different in your spiritual life. It takes a bit of focus, but a spiritual practice faithfully followed over time will yield to you all the Wisdom you could ever need, all the Peace you could ever want, and enough Love to heal you and everything around you.

When I say "spiritual practice," I mean the actions you take each day to return you to a sense of connection with your Divine Self, the part of you that is Love Herself, is Source, is All, is God Herself, is your Highest Self, is the Universe, is an Enlighted

Being, is Peace. What you call it does not matter, only that you do. It only matters that you figure out a way of connecting to that Source. Your spiritual practice is the things you do physically to allow you to access, cultivate, and manifest what you want to feel spiritually. And honestly, what's the difference between what you feel spiritually and physically? I don't think there is one.

I do not mean the casual tarot spread, or the meditation class you went to one time, or even that one retreat that allegedly transformed you and got you spiritually high. I'm not talking about the love and light, spiritual bypassing, whitewashed and commodified eastern religion you see on Instagram.

I'm talking about sitting your ass down for five minutes at the top of your day and breathing. I'm talking about intentional meditation and movement. I'm talking about learning to feel, honor, and let go of your feelings. I'm talking about grieving what you've lost in a way that will help you find what you want next. I'm talking about connecting with your ancestors. I'm talking about figuring out what your people believed before colonization. I'm talking about unpacking your privilege. I'm talking about taking responsibility for your own happiness and well-being. I'm talking about creating a sustainable thing you do every day that makes you feel so good that you can't wait to do it again the next day. I'm talking about the things you can do when you are so deep in the pit of despair that will light the way out. I'm talking about letting go of the shit that still hurts and doing what makes you come alive. I'm talking about what makes you bloom.

I'm talking about the real nuts and bolts of this spiritual stuff. And I will not lie to you, when you start your spiritual path, when you begin undoing all the toxic beliefs you've held just below the surface of your conscious mind, it feels hella painful. You will feel better, but you'll feel more of everything. This is slow work, and we're also so impatient with the process.

So many of us want magic, meaning we want something outside of us to fix us, and we want it to fix us now. We think it's in the programs and the books we read. We believe it's in our natal chart and the three crystals in our pocket right now, or if we can get the correct belief, if we can understand the proper theology, then we will feel good. It will all make sense when we accomplish being a good deconstructed person!

Here's what I wish I had known at the top of the journey: a bad theology will kill you, but a good theology will not save you because none of this is about right belief. It's not a program you finish, and you're certified whole. You are not broken. You are not evil to your core, needing to armor yourself with virtues to keep your evil juices from leaking out into a world that is also corrupt and bad for some reason. You don't need saving because you were never in danger. You don't need to get found because you've never been lost.

You've been asleep.
I'm here to gently wake you the fuck up.

What I am offering you is a practice that, when consistent, will lead you to clarity of mind, Peace in the Body, and hopefully a perspective that may bring some beautiful, luscious, floral poetry into the landscape of arid wilderness that has been your faith.

It is a practice to remind you daily that you are whole.
And it is You who will get yourself there.

If you've been wondering how to recover after spiritual abuse, after losing or having to leave your old spiritual community, after the church kicked you out,

If you've been desperate to feel that feeling you felt in those old spaces, the real connection you had with those real people,

If you've been angry about missing it or sad because you haven't found nearly anything as meaningful as that,

If you're ready to heal from that shit, this is for you.

This book shares with you the ideas and practices that finally led me to lay down a lot of my shit. I may introduce you to some seemingly new ideas, but none of it is original. I'm an amalgamation of great teachers, yogis, theologians, and practitioners, so know that we're standing on the shoulders of giants. Or perhaps we are standing among a great cloud of witnesses, with our great ancestors, alongside fully realized ones who help teach us what it is to remain and abide in Love.

For me, every moment comes back to one question, "What must I do to return to Peace?" I wait, listen, and then do what is presented to me. And then I evaluate. Did it bring me Peace? And if yes, I mark it as helpful. If not, I let it go.

Early on in my exploration, I tried on a lot of new ideas and practices. However, I kept returning to the same few things: stillness and movement.

Meditation and stilling my mind got me to a place where I could finally stop the anxiety of my conscious mind and drop into that Peace, and when I remembered it was possible to feel that, I could quickly return. The more I practiced that feeling of Peace, the more I committed myself to do things that kept me there, the more I remained in that feeling. Life seemed to blossom, and my problems seemed to shrink against the beauty of the world as I saw it with clear eyes, seeing how it worked together to keep everything, including me, alive and moving.

Learning to move my Body in ways that felt good was also a pathway toward greater levels of accepting all of me. I leaned into hatha yoga, lifted weights, and swore off stepping on scales because I no longer wanted my idea of health to be dictated by bullshit. I started taking walks, sitting outside, and listening to the trees. I took the same mindfulness I had on my meditation cushion into the rest of my work, the working out, and the relationships I was keeping.

> Peace. Even when shit was hitting the fan.
> Peace. Despite the fact I didn't know how I would get the bills paid.
> Peace. Before, during, and after the Trump White House.
> Peace. That passeth understanding.

The very last chapter of this book will offer some very practical how-to for creating your own practice, but every chapter between here and there will offer glimpses as well. But the essentials are already clear: stillness, presence, breath, and movement.

MIRACLES

One of the most significant changes in my life was finding *A Course in Miracles* (ACIM), a metaphysical text from 1975. Penned by the scribe Dr. Helen Schucman, ACIM gives a delicious theological discourse on living without separation from God, a workbook for students who wish to test the ideas out, and a manual for teachers who want to help others find their path back to God. One of the wacky things Dr. Schucman says is that this all came about when she heard a voice from within say, "This is a course in miracles. Take notes." And she did. And out popped this collection of texts. Oh, and the voice? She says it was Jesus Christ.

Yes. That Jesus Christ.

That made me pause and want to run and hide all at once. I didn't need another text or holy book. I'd just gotten over my authority problem with the Bible. I wasn't about to get indoctrinated into another bullshit cult. But ACIM proved to be different. It tells you explicitly that you don't have to believe any of it. It's all ideas on how to get back to God. In the manual for teachers, it says, "Give up what you do not want. Keep what you do."

ACIM also posited that I shouldn't believe anything anyone tells me but rather test everything for myself. I am the authority in my life. And I can see what Love is and what hate is. This book is only trying to get me to believe that God loves me and that, in reality, I am one with God. And that's not so bad, I suppose.

Another suggestion ACIM gave me that I have given to all my students is to stop looking for what is True with a capital T. Stop asking whether or not beliefs are true. Ask if they are helpful. Make helpfulness the criteria for any idea that enters your head as to whether or not you hold on to it.

In this book, I reference ACIM quite a bit because those principles have helped me undo all the final bits of fear I had of God and allowed me to enter into Peace. It's not a book for everyone, but it can be transformative for those who it is for. It reframes all the theology I grew up with in a practical way that allows me to experience the reality that I never left heaven. Even the idea of a miracle becomes an everyday occurrence. "A miracle is a shift in perception from fear to love—from a belief in what is not real, to faith in that which is. That shift in perception changes everything."

The last element from ACIM that I'll highlight here is that we teach what we want to learn. As my spiritual practice grew, I wanted to learn how to do this more. I liked this feeling of God's presence, Love's power buzzing in me all the time. And what I realized still is that these spiritual highs and the ecstatic oneness that I was beginning to experience were not the point. I wasn't any less in Love when I was angry or bored than I was when I was on the yoga mat or in deep meditation. Those moments are meant to show us what Love feels like, what Peace feels like, and how it is always Here. It is always Now.

So I showed other people what I was doing. I began coaching folks and leading them through mediative practices on these ideas that would come to me. I shared many of the ideas I found in esoteric texts, the religious books of many faiths, and from other theologians and practitioners, all with the caveat that you didn't have to like it or even keep what I was suggesting. I just presented an idea of God's unending Love being present in all things and asked if it could be true. My ultimate job was, and still is, keeping myself in the center of Love and holding space for others to expand into this same generous space.

After I completed my master's degree in practical theology, I began working with groups of people, seeing if these unique ideas could work in community. If these practices would benefit others in the same way they helped me. The question I was asking was, "Does this shit work?"

And by and large, the answer was yes.

I kept refining my methods, kept learning, and took dozens of folks through processes of discovering some authentic and profound spiritual practices and a journey of changing their minds about who they were, what Love is, and where their lives could go with that knowledge.

This book is one of what I hope will be many expressions and ideas of what faith, spirituality, and practice can be for so many of us going forward. I hope this book will be the miracle that so many of you have been waiting for, the thing that will help you shift your mind from fear to love.

A LIVING PRACTICE: A CREATIVE PATH FOR REDISCOVERING WHAT MAKES YOU BLOOM

As I was putting words to the feelings, practices, and pathways I have crafted for myself, I realized that all that lofty stuff, that yummy, luscious, delicious, spiritual mumbo jumbo is well and good if you have a taste of it already. Still, some of us are also starting from scratch. I firmly believe that good theology is only as good as it is helpful, and the best kind of theology is practical. It can be lived out and tested. I'm sharing the things I have tried and found to be exceedingly helpful in helping me, and others, return to Peace.

Finish this sentence.
For the fruit of the Spirit is . . .

If you can finish that sentence, you've got religious trauma.
If you can't, go read your Bible, you heathen.

Kidding.

Anyway, the Bible says that the fruit of the Spirit is Love, Joy, Peace, Patience, Kindness, Generosity, Faithfulness, Gentleness, and Self-Control.

Love it. Gorgeous. So what?

Growing up, this was an arbitrary list of qualities we just threw around. Some of these virtues were clearly defined, like Self-Control and Gentleness. The first three, Love, Joy, and Peace, were always skipped over because I think the people preaching on this verse had no idea how to approach them because they had little Peace in their lives. Let alone Joy or Love.

I love this verse because it clearly lists what naturally happens when one is in Love. These are not things you can do. These are qualities you develop. They are fruits that you pick off the tree and take a bite of. You enjoy these things after planting, growing, developing, rain and shine, bugs eating the leaves, frost, and heat-wave, and *then!*

Then bloom.

Then harvest.

But maybe you don't know the processes of developing these virtues or attitudes within yourself. Perhaps you have no idea how to make these things bloom in your life, let alone what makes you bloom. You don't have the techniques for growing this shit or the seed. Plus, the soil is hard as fuck. It feels like it's been too long. Like nothing good could grow here.

Beloved, I need you to trust me on this one: you are not a lost cause. And if you practice even a fraction of what I present to you in this book, your life will change. So grab your spiritual overalls, tools, and a huge sun hat 'cause we've got work to do.

I call this process that helps you rediscover what makes you bloom Creating a Living Practice. It will help till the soil of your heart so that these seeds might fall on good soil, and you may be able to maintain an environment conducive to your growth. The idea is that each fruit of the Spirit has a beginning point, a seed. The seed is the practice you keep, the thing you do each day, allowing you to enter into your awareness of Love's presence. This is the pathway toward finding our way back to Love, God, and Heaven because it shows us we never left. We just forgot.

Each chapter discusses a different principle or seed that, in time, blooms in the most delicious and unexpected ways, eventually bearing the fruit.

Practice blooms into Rhythm, which in time bears Self-Control.

Rest blooms into Imagination, easily creating Gentleness.

Willingness blooms into Devotion, which develops Faithfulness.

Friendship blooms into Solidarity, which flows into Generosity.

Radical honesty blooms into Defenselessness, which proves to be Kindness.

Unbearable Compassion blooms into Boundaries, which allows for Patience.

Surrender blooms into Forgiveness, and this brings Peace.

Acceptance blooms into grief, which in time turns into Joy. Pleasure blooms into Wonder, which sends us headlong into Love.

The following chapters will lead you through some new ideas, some delicious theopoetics, and at the end of each chapter, I will give you a set of mantras (short statements that sum up each chapter and can be used in meditation), some things to think about, some things to try, and a guided meditation that will help these ideas take root in your soul.

In the final chapter, I will provide a detailed outline for how to implement these practices in your life.

I know my ego is also already asking, "How much work will this take? How much effort?" Not much. You could read this book and not do any of the offered practices, and the ideas would still be helpful. But if you want to get these ethereal ideas out of your head and into your bones and your Body so you feel better, then your willingness to try is required.

This book will have some great theology (if I do say so myself), but a theology not embodied is just theory. Reading this book might give you some good ideas, but until your Body internalizes these better ideas, you will be someone with many good ideas that you don't believe at all. You deserve to feel good, to feel better, and to be free.

If you are new to meditation and mindfulness work, please do not worry and do not put the book down and walk away just because you think you can't do this. Trust me. You can. If you feel like you can't because your mind is too busy, I'd say you can't afford not to learn this.

I'm asking you something big here. I am asking you to trust me. I may ask you to do things that will undoubtedly make you uncomfortable. Please try them anyway.

THE BIG CAVEAT

There's one last thing I'd like to share with you before we begin:

I don't want you to believe anything I tell you.

Just because I have a degree, a larger following, and a sassy attitude doesn't mean I'm closer to God than you. I am like you. The only difference is that I've thought about this for a long while. The only difference is time and consistent practice. You'd feel this woo-woo, too, if you spent almost every day meditating on holy mysteries for the last five years.

On the real: this shit is difficult to write about. It's hard to write about touching the mystery of the soul. It's hard to explain to someone what Peace feels like. It's wordless. Love's presence is beyond what I could describe, even with perfect poetry. I believe that this is something you need to experience for yourself. I can't show you this. I can only share my experiences and practices in hopes that something that works for me works for you, with the recognition that what I offer is what has been offered to me and has worked for anyone willing.

My words will not teach you. No one's words have ever taught you. Your experience has always taught you. You must experience Peace to know what the hell I'm talking about. And it is possible.

I do not speak as someone throwing you platitudes or trying to get you to believe anything. I'm talking to you about my experience. I've done this shit, and I won't ask you to do something I am unwilling to do myself. And it may feel like I'm trying to offend you, and I'm not attempting to do that, I swear. I'm just presenting an idea. That's it. It could be wrong! But I'm willing to be wrong. And that makes everything easier.

I don't care what you believe. I care about how you feel and want you to feel good because that is how we save the world. When we feel good, we are more capable than when we are not feeling our best. I'm not trying to ignore your suffering. I want you to care enough about your suffering to attempt to end it.

Please, do not take my word for it, for anything. When you are given a new idea, please test it out. See if it's true for you. Not true for me, or your mama, or your bestie. You.

Try on these ideas as you try on a jacket or dress or some new denim. How does it feel on your Body? Does it fit well? Do you like it? And if it doesn't work, take it off. Get a different cut or size, or just take it off.

Start there. Get spiritually naked now. Drop all your concepts and ideas. Put it all on the table and ask, "Is this helpful? What does this belief, this practice, these relationships, this perspective, this desire, this concept, this religion, what is it doing in me, for me, to me, with me, through me?" Evaluate everything anyone says, including you and me, and let it all be questioned.

Question every thought that causes you pain. Welcome every thought that fills you with bliss. Inquire into all concepts that cause internal strife, grief, guilt, and shame. Embrace every thought that brings you closer to the awareness of Love's presence in all things.

One more thing: I recommend that you do not blitz through this book. This work is slow. It has to be for reasons that will become clear. If I may ask this of you, please do not read more than one chapter a day. Let the words and practices sink in. Listen to the meditations that accompany each chapter. Try the practices as recommended before improvising.

And finally, do not think this book will save your life. You will be doing that. But salvation is slow work, babe. Don't be in a hurry to get there. Be Here Now with me. Enjoy this process. It's going to be so much fun.

I love you so much. I'm glad you're here with me.

So, with a deep breath, let's begin.

MANTRAS FOR LEARNING WHAT MAKES YOU BLOOM

I am in touch with the Wisdom of my Body.
I am ready to let go of anything that is unhelpful.
I am rooted in my Divine Self.
I am willing to find what makes me Bloom.

THINGS TO THINK ABOUT:

♦ What were the spiritual practices you were taught growing up?

♦ Do you know what the beliefs of your people, your ancestors, were before Christianity? Before colonization and empire? This may require you to do a little research.

♦ How do you feel about spiritual practices now? Anxious? Excited? Fearful? Motivated?

- How does your Body feel right now? Tight or at ease? How's your breathing? Shallow or deep?

- Do some imagination work: Close your eyes and look into the future for a moment. Imagine your life in three months or so. You've been keeping your spiritual practices. You're shaking off the things that aren't helpful to you. What does this future version of you feel like? What are you doing differently?

THINGS TO TRY:

Listen to the first meditation I created for this book. Go to thekevingarcia.com/bloommeditations to listen for free.

1 | FEEL YOUR WAY BACK
On Practice, Rhythm, and Self-Control

> Come celebrate with me that everyday something has
> tried to kill me and has failed.
> —Lucille Clifton, "Won't You Celebrate with Me"

When I was a kid, maybe ten or eleven, my grandfather asked
me if I wanted to go to the Promise Keepers conference with him
and the other men of the church. I don't know why I agreed or
why anyone thought it was appropriate for me to go to something
like this, but you can be assured that I lowered the average age by
at least twenty years.

Even at that tender age, I was aware that I didn't quite
measure up to what it meant to be a man. I was effeminate, loved
performing, and had all the classic gay mannerisms (broken wrist,
a slight lilt in my voice, and so on). This made me the perfect
candidate for something like Promise Keepers. I think maybe
my uncle (who was our pastor) and grandfather thought this
would help me. Or perhaps save them from whatever impending
faggotry would blossom in me later. Who knows! This is where I
learned that I should make my Body my slave.

The Spirit is willing, but the flesh is weak. That was
hammered home all weekend. We heard testimonies from guys

who had been porn addicts and nearly ruined their lives and their marriages, but then Jesus saved them. And then God told them to download Covenant Eyes or XXXChurch's spyware programs to keep them accountable to their wives.

At this conference, I became terrified of the homosexual agenda because, on some level, I knew he was talking about me. I knew I was different and the kind of person the gays would "try to recruit." I heard the testimony of men who "got out of the lifestyle" and found wives. Being a little zealot, baptized at age nine, I wept at the reality of my sin. I wanted to be measured, good, and a man after God's heart. Whatever these feelings were, I must learn to control them. This is discipline. This is Self-Control.

Don't drink. Don't smoke. Don't cuss. Don't have sex until after you are in a heterosexual marriage. Don't watch those movies. Don't gamble. Don't hang out with sinners unless you're going to evangelize them. Don't think about sex. Don't think about gay sex, especially. Don't think about masturbating. And definitely don't think about the porn you watched last week when you promised you'd never do it again, and now you're feeling bad about doing it again . . .

As it was taught to us, Self-Control was about punishment and deprivation. We have all these natural cravings as humans for sex, food, and comfort, and we are taught to punish them all. You should only want one thing, and that's God. And God wants all this shit that makes you feel miserable, but count it all as Joy because it won't even matter when you stand in glory!

Self-Control was taught to us to manage the minds of the population, getting us to hold on to certain beliefs and therefore continue specific actions. Something they got right was tuning in to the fact that everything begins in the mind with the beliefs we hold. If we believe that we are shitty, broken, and evil to our core, then everything that flows from that will somehow embody that notion. If we think the opposite, that we are God's Wonder, fully made, fully incarnate, here with a purpose of joyful, conscious cocreation, then . . . I mean, what could happen? I imagine something beautiful.

When I think of the most self-controlled people, I think of folks who are measured. I think of people who never feel pressured to do the things that make them feel less than loved. I think of folks who take action when they need to and step back when they want. I don't think of people who deny themselves for the sake of complaining about how hard it is to deny the thing they want. That's not giving something up for the sake of liberation. That's just producing a bunch of horny celibates.

I'd like to posit that Self-Control has nothing to do with the things you don't do and everything to do with doing only what you want to do and nothing more. It's getting rid of shoulds and have-tos. It's letting go of guilt-ridden action and asking, once again, what will feel good. What will return me to Peace? To God? To Self?

Think of Self-Control with a capital S, Self. When I say Self with a capital S, I mean the part of you that is Soul, God, the creative force that creates and sustains the Universe, the same power that raised Christ from the dead, the breath that enters your lungs . . . I mean your true Self, who You are before the stories you tell about yourself. That Self—What if that Self was in control? What if your Peace was the thing guiding you instead of your panic? What if it was the Spirit of Love over the Spirit of Fear? Your right mind over your ego? Use whatever language you want; just recognize that when you are at Peace, when you are aware of Love, when you are aware of Self, you can move from that place with extreme clarity.

That is what you need. Forget needing to predict the future. You need to get clarity about the Here and Now. If you get that right, you will have everything you need for whatever comes next.

As I said in the intro, these are fruits of the Spirit. Meaning they come after the process. They are things you pick off the vine and sink your teeth into. Self-Control is the result of the way you conduct your life. And the way you conduct your life is your practice.

But where do we begin with practice? There are a zillion different things out here past the edges of our former faith. How do we start?

With our breath.

FEEL YOUR WAY BACK: FINDING PRACTICE

Take a second and breathe in deeply. Exhale completely. Notice what's going on in your Body, even as you've been reading these first few thousand words. What emotions have you felt? What stories have begun swirling? What does your Body feel like right now? For a moment, mentally scan your physical Self. Notice where you might be holding tension. Is there anything you can release or loosen?

Take another deep breath in. Exhale completely. One more time in. And out.

For just a minute, close your eyes and just turn your view inward. Ask your Body, "How are we doing?" And listen for what they might say. If you aren't hearing anything, use your imagination. If your Body had a voice to communicate with words instead of feelings, how would they describe how they feel?

This is imagination work. It allows your Body to speak through the only avenue you can hear: through your silence and attention.

Set the book down and just stay here for a few more breaths. Notice how good it feels to slow down and not do anything for a second, to just be Here and Now.

Or, maybe this was hella uncomfortable. Notice that too. Often when we begin new things like paying attention to the Body after ignoring it like we have been trained to, it is startling. We feel the fears and anxieties well up and our programming kicking in. "Can't stop! Don't wanna feel bad feelings! Gotta keep working! Gotta keep moving! Eventually, I'll be okay!"

You can be okay right now. You *are* okay right now. Other than your thoughts and feelings about your thoughts and feelings, are you alright? You just need to stay just a bit longer. You don't need to go anywhere. It's normal to want to run from stillness. But see if you can just stay a bit longer. Hear your Body saying to you, "Be with me. Linger here just a bit longer. I've got you."

Trust me, this part doesn't last forever. (And if that was hard, stick with me until the end of the chapter. There's a guided meditation waiting for you.)

Thích Nhất Hạnh, one of the most distinguished Zen masters and meditation teachers of our lifetime, said that when we are mindful of the breath, the in and the out, our mind and Body become the same thing. And that is huge because how often is that the case for you? How often do you feel a sense of oneness with your Self in the Here and Now? How frequently do you feel the Peace that passes understanding well up from within? Conversely, how often do you feel uptight? Uneasy? How easily are you triggered or knocked off your center? How often are you in fear, and how often are you in Love?

When we slow our breath, we also inevitably slow the thoughts in our minds. They are like children who just need a break from overstimulation. Your breath and attention do this. On a somatic level (somatic means on the embodied level, what's happening without your conscious mind's direction), deep breathing tells the Body it's safe to slow down. Our amygdala, the part of our brain responsible for our quick fight/flight/freeze/fawn responses, is taken out of the driver seat. Panic subsides. And what arises in its place is Wisdom. What we realize is that under the storm of our own thoughts, on the other side of a stilled breath, is the Peace that we've been so desperate for the whole time.

And that Peace you conjured up? You did that. You turned your attention to something already present, always present within. And all it took was a deep breath and a few moments of focus. Isn't that interesting? How simple was that! This is the presence of Wisdom. The mind at Peace is the presence of the Holy Spirit.

Now, do it again, but do it for a minute. Then maybe five minutes. And then perhaps do that every day. Just to see what happens.

And then you nod, and we both smile, and you go off into the rest of your life. Life happens, and you forget. You don't meditate tomorrow. And you'll say, "That's okay. I'll do it tomorrow."

But beloved, I caution you against tomorrow. If you want Peace now, you should go for it now. Your practice doesn't need to be perfect. It doesn't need to be formal. It doesn't need to be elaborate. But consistency is the only thing that yields life-changing results, and unfortunately, we've been consistent in all the wrong ways because of our training.

We've been trained to over-function. We've been trained to think that hard work will give us what we want: comfort and Peace. We've been taught to not pay attention to our feelings because feelings are not suitable for capitalism's schemes. Mental health is not a concern, nor is the health of the Body. What we are doing here is retraining ourselves. Don't think about unlearning anything; instead, turn your attention to what works.

In meditation, we are turning our minds toward the Peace that exists already, the Love that is already present. Meditation is practicing the feeling of Peace. One should make it a point to focus on the feelings generated in meditation and how it feels to feel good. Because if you can remember what it feels like, returning to it becomes so much more straightforward. Meditation is practice for the rest of your day. Spending even five minutes at the top of your day reconnecting with your Divine Self will allow your most authentic Self to guide you throughout the day.

And . . . beloved, that's it.
That's the whole thing.
That's the goal right there.
I wanna feel at Peace right now.
I wanna be in Love right now. And I am.
I just have to remember.

I forgot because something happened that took my attention away from it, but right now, as soon as I notice, let me remember. Let me return to my breath. Let me take a moment to recalibrate and recenter. Not because anger is wrong, not because stress is a sin, and not because we shouldn't feel impermissible feelings, but because I want to feel better. Sometimes the emotion takes a long time to pass. Sometimes I'm so bogged down and sad or depressed or grieving something or someone I've lost.

That's wonderful. This is the time to do it. Whatever feelings or emotions come up, they don't need to be explained away or destroyed. They need to be cared for. They need your compassion. And they came to you because they knew you could not fail them. These parts of you are begging to be seen. Meditation is beginning to witness all the things we've carried, all the splintered selves that have been quietly suffering within and becoming whole again.

THE ANATOMY OF BELIEF

Wow, that sounds awful, Kevin. Is there a less painful option?

What's interesting is you have been carrying this pain inside for so long. You've learned to tolerate it. You've learned to be okay with constantly betraying yourself to the point you think it's normal. You are dealing with your emotions in a way that you spend a ton of energy containing them, keeping them at bay, rather than letting them flow through you. Imagine what it would be like to not have to manage all your hard emotions, all your impermissible feelings that you've been actively ignoring, and just release them. Imagine if your mind wasn't always so occupied with keeping these thoughts or feelings away. What might that be like?

That's what's waiting for you on the other side of your practice, your quieted thoughts, and your stilled breath. It will not happen all at once. You may feel overwhelmed, but most everything feels overwhelming when doing it for the first time.

Trust me on this. Stick to your breath. Stick to your small daily things. And sooner than you think, you'll begin to see your reactions and inner world shift in the most beautiful ways.

Your feelings are a guide for you. They aren't a nuisance. They are telling you, at any given moment, whether the thought you are holding in your mind, conscious or unconscious, is aligned with what your Self knows to be true. If you feel discord, anxiety, or fear, it might be because you believe something untrue. If you feel Joy, Peace, or happiness, it could be that you believe something wonderful.

And what is a belief? Abraham Hicks says that a belief is just a thought you keep having over and over again. We have clung so tightly in the past to rigid beliefs, meaning we forced ourselves to think a certain way under penalty of eternal damnation. The longer a thought lives within us, the more momentum it gains, and the harder it seems to slow it down, let alone be able to get off it. But, my friend, it is possible to undo those thoughts, to find better, more helpful beliefs that get you closer to experiencing your Divine Self.

And that should be your test. Don't ask if something is true. Ask if something is helpful. Let's use this example that kept me trapped for so long.

"Being gay is a sin."

That was my big one. I held that thought in my head, and it felt terrible because I could never live with it. And I wasn't allowed to have a different thought because to think differently was a sin. It did nothing but keep me small and make me think that God didn't love me. It made me think God hated me. But then, I was introduced to a different idea.

"God made Queer people on purpose."

It was intriguing. It was scary. Because it meant that all the assumptions and fears I held up for so long were just . . . wrong. I was wrong. I'd been wrong for so long, yet I was trained to think that to separate from what my authority figures taught was to be separated from God. So what should I do?

My advice is the same as before. Test it out. Test everything. Who are you with and without each of these thoughts? What fills you with fear and dismay? What fills you with hope and possibly intrigue? Which thoughts are helpful? Which thoughts aren't?

Love is obvious. So is hate. Stop acting like this is hard to understand and start trusting your Body. Changing your beliefs is as easy as changing your mind, and the reality is that change can only occur on the level of thought. Once that is healed, everything else naturally aligns with your most authentic Self.

But no way it's that simple. I just sit here for a little bit and breathe, and it's gonna what? Make me feel better? Connect me to God? How's thinking about thinking gonna do shit for me?

I love that you asked.

There's this story from the Bhagavad Gita where Krishna, the Divine manifestation and voice for God on earth, is driving his chariot and his student, Arjuna, and listening to him complain. Arjuna lists off all the things he doesn't want to do and his woes. He is freaking out about the state of the world he finds himself in. He is overwhelmed, and finally, he talks and talks and talks and talks so much that he exhausts all his words. Overcome with grief and despair, Arjuna asks his teacher to tell him what to do and then falls silent.

And then, with a smirk, Krishna begins to teach him about the nature of all reality. He looks at his student and says he speaks as if he has Wisdom, but the wise do not mourn for the living nor the dead, for they know the nature of the soul is eternal, passing into another form after this one is finished. Krishna talks about the cycle of death and rebirth, which is a delicious story, but I want us to notice what happens before Arjuna gets the help he needs.

Arjuna stops. He becomes silent. He shuts the fuck up finally and lets Wisdom speak from the silence.

Arjuna knows that he doesn't know what to do. He's tried everything. He's even been a student of Krishna's for a while. He is a devout seeker, not just some fool who has been idle. He's been a good religious person, following this teacher of God, seeking to learn and become enlightened. And even the religious person, who is face-to-face with his guru, still had to come to stillness before his teacher would speak. Before he could hear what to do, he had to stop and be ready to receive.

This is the same way we must approach our practice. We must be at a point of giving up the other stuff that we know doesn't work. We must stop comparing now to then. We need, in a way, to be exhausted enough to stop. We need to fail at what we've tried before sometimes before we are willing to try something else. We need to be willing to ask for help before it comes.

Truth is, you don't *need* a teacher or a practice. If you understood your connection to Love and Love as the only reality, you probably wouldn't be reading this book. If you were in constant, uninterrupted connection to God, I'd be asking you for help. So we find the practices and the teachers to help us.

The practices found in this book are a great place to start. Don't see it as a rule book but a guidebook to help you look for signposts within yourself. And! I recommend trying the practices as suggested first. The reason is, no offense, you probably don't have any idea what you're doing, do you?

Or maybe you've got some idea, but it hasn't produced any lasting results for you, has it?

The spiritual buffet we have at our fingertips is a blessing and a curse of our modern world. With the internet and social media, spiritualism, new-age ideas, and the classic appropriation of nonwhite Indigenous cultures, there's a never-ending supply of ideas to draw from. Seekers leaving their faith tradition will begin by trying to do everything and sustain everything. They pull from many traditions and end up with a field of potholes, none significantly deep and none hitting the water.

There's a great gift in the multiplicity of ideas we have; it is your job to discern which path to take and which hole to dig deeper. And you've got to stay in it long enough for it to work on you. You need to probe the depths of your own heart.

This is another excellent reason I think having a spiritual director or a teacher can be incredibly beneficial. Having someone walking alongside you as you go through your dark night of the soul, as the hard feelings come up and you want to quit, as you have all the doubts that come with an expanding faith, is just so freaking helpful.

A good teacher will always point the power back to you. The teacher is not your path to God. They are just the person showing you the "shortcuts," so to speak. They are helping speed you up a little bit and get you into the receiving mode, but ultimately, they are holding up a mirror so you can see what binds you, and so you can untie yourself from these binds.

You cannot rely on another person's faith or practice to sustain you. This is what we did in church all those years. We showed up every Sunday and drank in the worship music. We feasted on the fancy words from the pastor. And then we spiritually starved all week because we had no idea how to generate those feelings outside that space. So we went back, and we repeated the cycle. We learned to be codependent on churches, needing their approval of our path and practice.

Trying to live into someone else's path brings great fear and pain. Trying to be someone you are not brings terrible suffering. The way to avoid this is by establishing yourself in a regular rhythm of practice that you begin incorporating, committing to, and allowing to change you.

VIBES: FINDING RHYTHM

Practice, pursued with willingness and earnestness, blooms into glorious new life rhythms. The things we do, the way we speak, and the paths we walk change for the better. As you make your Peace your priority without apology, your world becomes more gorgeous.

As you get into these new practices, these new thought patterns begin to take shape, and then new life begins to form. You'll notice how your personal rhythms start to shift. One way is that feeling good becomes normal. Feeling a sense of ease and well-being is part of your living experience, and as you realize this is the default, you'll not be able to tolerate anything less.

Said another way: Peace is the default setting of our nature. Stress management is our failing strategy. Stop managing your stress and let the fuck go.

New rhythms bring new dance partners too. The people you connect with, those you vibe with, will likely be different. This doesn't mean better, but hopefully, you will be learning what feels good to you by now. Hopefully, you're not relying on others' healing to work on your own healing. You'll start noticing what's sucking your energy and giving you life, and you'll naturally want to gravitate to what makes you bloom.

Noticing what is out of sync with your newfound Peace can be jarring at first because while sometimes it's a habit you need to drop, other times (a lot of the time, honestly) it's people who are out of step with your current life. What's worse is if you come from high-pressure, super-conservative religious, and/or code-pendent spaces, one person moving toward health and freedom spells trouble for the group. Even if the behaviors are incredibly unhealthy, those in unhealthy environments or organizations, be it churches or families, will seek to push you back into behaviors and relationships to keep you small.

What you do next is up to you. Will you shrink back to who you were before? Will you delay your Joy? Will you push back your pleasure to keep these relationships, the circumstances, to keep your life from changing again? Even though it's been making you miserable?

At first, it feels so hard to say no to the people and things we've always been connected to. It feels mean. It feels harsh. And beloved, let it be hard. Let it be uncomfortable because what's more painful than saying no to something you think you should do is saying yes to something you don't want to do.

As much as possible, don't take the discomfort so seriously. It'll pass. People might get mad, and that is really interesting, isn't it? They are getting angry that you are doing something you want. They are getting upset because they can't rely on you the same way they used to because you are prioritizing your feeling good. And is that such a bad thing?

Early in your spiritual recovery, as you begin to cultivate a living practice, I think it's imperative to surround yourself with people supporting your growth and freedom, limiting time with folks who have historically been a drag on your soul. Our tender heart needs space to heal and grow strong before facing all the onslaughts we've met and walked through. We must learn what it is to be soft without letting go of the ground we've gained.

We must learn to stay rooted. And the way we do this is through, you guessed it, practice.

You must practice doing only what you want, only what makes you bloom. Don't think about not doing something. Don't think about not saying certain words. Think about what you could do that would make you feel good. Do that. Think about the poetry that really stirs your soul. Read that. Think about the places that feel like home. Go there. Think about the people who make you come alive. Hang out with them.

Let your loyalty lie with you and your Body first. Seek first the Kingdom, the awareness of Love in every moment, and everything else will be taken care of.

WHAT I WANT: REALIZING SELF-CONTROL

Be aware of your one goal, the one thing you are after.

Love.

You're desiring and going after a sense of connection to the Divine. With that connection, in that place of Peace and affirmation, all things are possible. We can do everything we wish and feel empowered to say no to things we don't want. We learn that what we want is an equilibrium of Spirit and Body. We move away from suffering and things that cause others to suffer as a natural consequence of being connected to Love.

This is what Self-Control truly is. It is letting my Highest Self, the part of me that is Love, be in control. It is letting my Peace be my guide. It is letting my breath be my grounding. It isn't about staying away from anything or not doing stuff. There is merit if fasting for spiritual revelation, but there is no merit in the deprivation of the Body as a means to attain Holiness.

You are holy. Your Holiness blesses this world and everything you see. Who you are is Holiness. And you don't have to believe that, but you'd be indescribably happy if you did.

That one thought that I am part of God's mind and very holy reminds me that my baseline isn't evil but Goodness. I'm not working to cover myself in virtue and good works. I'm sitting still to remember the Holiness of my true Self. The seed within me, the core within me, the deposit of the Godself, is who I truly am. Nothing to stop or peel off or push away. Nothing to shrink or decrease so that God may increase, but instead, I must let that most authentic part of me expand past the stories I tell about myself. I must increase, shine brighter, and come alive if God is to be known in me.

This idea of oneness with God expands beyond my thought life. Once my mind is healed, the rest of my experience follows suit. As you have more delicious thoughts about your Self and your life, your outlook and attitude change. Your Body feels better because you are not stressing out, focusing on the things keeping you trapped. It's a very subtle shift, but it makes all the difference. And this good feeling, noticing what is helping and what it's doing for us, keeps us coming back.

Self-Control is allowing our Divine Self to lead. It is relearning how easy it is to be at one with ourselves. It is being deliberately gentle with the entire process and all the emotions and feelings that come with it.

If you keep your practices, the tiny things that turn into life rhythms, you will find that Self-Control leads you directly into ease and comfort, into Gentleness. You realize there is so much you don't have to do. There is rest to be had. Stay here.

CREATE THE SPACE

We are physical beings. We are creatures who love symbols and rituals. There's a reason we gravitate to things like churches or to the woo-woo. How you shape your new practice should be no different. Before, we had symbols and rituals. We just didn't call them that. The bread and the cup, the communion table, those were huge. They were both the symbol of salvation and of belonging to a community. Gathering for candlelight services around Christmastime. Sunrise services for Easter. Bible studies. Small groups. All of those things were part of our practice. And perhaps if you're reading this book, you're at a place where those things are now inaccessible for one reason or another. Sacred space seems off-limits to us now.

But the sacred space is within you. Do not believe the lie that you must go somewhere and do something with someone to feel your innate connection to your Divine Self. You will begin to feel it so quickly, and the more intentional you are about this, the more likely it will happen sooner.

One way to make your practice more intentional is to set a space aside in your home, your apartment, or your room that is expressly set aside for seated practice. The reason we make a physical space is to remind us of what already exists within us, to remind us of what is true and real. It can become a safe place to fully fall apart and fully come alive. Seated practice is your time of meditation and stillness, precisely without anything else. No tarot cards or chanting. Quiet contemplation with the intention of connecting with Source.

From a physical standpoint, setting aside a sacred space and creating a small altar gives the mind and Body something to focus on. It helps cue the Body and brain to prepare for stillness. From a metaphysical standpoint, creating a sacred space with an altar gives you the freedom to begin working out your shit. It gives you a starting point for practice; energetically, you are taking time to clear out whatever isn't helping you anymore. In some way, it says to the Universe, "I am open to getting help from something outside myself." Or better yet, "I am willing to go deep within to find the Wisdom available at all times."

An altar can go from elaborate to very simple. It could consist of a few crystals you've picked up at the botanica, a candle, and maybe a picture of a saint, teacher, or holy person you still admire. It could be a picture of people you love who have died and are still with you. It could be a miniature statue of the Buddha you've got from that one time you were in Asia on that mission trip. It doesn't matter the form. What matters is whether or not you give it meaning.

The altar is a space to engage with your subtle energies, make space for your emotions, and ask your angels, guides, ancestors, and/or God to help make you aware of Love's presence. When I began creating these sacred spaces for myself, it consisted of my tarot cards, a few crystals, the scented candle I got at Kroger earlier that day, and my journal.

Every day, before I started, I would sit and breathe for a minute or till my Body felt calm. I pulled a few cards, asking, "What do I need to pay attention to today?" And then I'd journal about the cards. I'd say thank you to my Body, for keeping me going. I'd say thank you to God, for guiding me. I'd say thank you to the Earth, for continuing to let us all continue. And then I'd go work at that shit restaurant job.

Nothing too elaborate. I didn't have a devotional practice with anyone then, and I certainly wasn't talking to Jesus right off the bat. I had to warm up to the idea that Jesus wasn't the white imitation colonizer I was fooled into following for so long but rather my brother and friend if I wanted him to be.

It is now your task to create a sacred space for yourself in whatever way you can. Setting aside space in your home for your practice is excellent. In my own house, I turned my office into a meditation room. Before that, I had a coffee table in my living room in front of an open window with gorgeous light coming in with my altar set up. Before that, it was a small desk in my one-bedroom apartment at seminary. Before that, I shared the top of my dresser in my room with another grown-ass human. All that to say, there is nothing too small. What matters is that you can go there and be comfortable. Even your bedside table can become a sacred space.

By creating an altar space where you live, you begin to give yourself a visual reminder that there's more to life than what's on the surface. You begin to remind yourself that you can return to your practice anytime to find Peace. It is a physical practice that will start to change you spiritually.

When you create sacred space for yourself, you learn to slow down. You remember the sacred art of rest. And your rest practice will truly begin to save your life.

BEGIN TO NOTICE

I tell my students to begin with very small devotional practices. No more than a few minutes each day. People usually scratch their head and ask, "That's it?" Yes. We do not want to change so quickly, and in fact, we can't. We're so practiced in one direction, to try and drastically change our thought patterns so quickly feels like too much. So we go slow. We take it easy. We tend to go too hard in the West in just about every way. We aren't used to taking things slow, or for processes being easy. It's that sacrifice bullshit again. We think that a practice has to be hard or it's not working. It has to hurt a little bit for me to know that it's helping. And the thing is, it hurts sometimes, but only because we realize we've been holding on to the painful for so long.

What happens very quickly after keeping your practice is you begin to notice your emotions. You notice your Body more. You feel everything more. So yes, you will feel better, but you will also likely begin to feel all the stuff you've been repressing. You'll maybe be sadder for a bit as you recognize what you've been missing. You must grieve for the life you'll never have. And on the other side of that, there is Peace.

As you begin to notice more, you are more able to respond how you want to, rather than unconsciously reacting to your triggers. The first time it happens, when you notice that you didn't blow up the way you thought you would, when you recognize that you didn't start yelling or crying when having that hard conversation, when you realize how much control you really do have over your energies . . . it feels so good. A cute little pride rises up when you realize that this is Self-Control.

You at your core, when the troubles of the world are not as heavy, when you are regularly meditated and keeping a rhythm of life that feels good, you recognize that who You are is someone who is naturally self-controlled. No need to try. It is just a natural result of you keeping to a regular practice. And isn't that just dope? Here you were, just doing something tiny to make yourself feel good, and for whatever reason, you are able to navigate the rest of your life with a level of clarity and ease you've never had before! Except there is a reason.

You've practiced. You've practiced the feeling of Peace. You've practiced the thoughts that lead you toward a sense of Love. Congrats! You've done it.

That's the whole thing babe. And what's so lovely is that your Self-Control is what leads you effortlessly into a practice of rest. And as you rest, you begin to recognize even more who you are.

You're remembering who you are, beloved. And doesn't it feel so very good to be who you are?

MANTRAS FOR FEELING YOUR WAY BACK

My feelings and emotions are data.
I'm willing to do what it takes to feel good today.

I respond to all my feelings with deep compassion and understanding.
There's nothing stopping me from loving myself.

THINGS TO THINK ABOUT:

- ◆ What was my practice before? Was there any part of it that I enjoyed or connected with?

- ◆ When I think of Holiness, do I think of my Self? Why or why not?

- ◆ What has stopped me from creating new practices up to this point?

- ◆ Are there people in my life who are also on this journey with whom I can share this?

- ◆ What's one thing I can do daily, or even something I can do right now, that would make me feel better?

THINGS TO TRY:

1. Create a sacred altar space for your spiritual practice in your home, as suggested in this chapter. (You can also google a zillion different ways. Find the one that feels good to you and go for it.)

2. Meditate for one minute, on the hour, between 9 a.m. and 9 p.m. As you meditate, note your thoughts and how they make you feel. If they cause you to stress or suffer, gently question them, asking, "Is that true?" (For step-by-step instructions on creating a sustainable practice, check out chapter 10.)

3. This is an adaptation from an idea Byron Katie gives in her book *Loving What Is*. Take yourself for a walk every day without any technology. Look at the world as if you've never seen anything before. In your mind, keep asking, "What is it?" As you go along, begin to name things very simply. "Tree. Car. House. Sun. Sky." And perhaps as you go along, you just call it all "beautiful." See what happens.

4. Make a list of ten things that would feel really good or fun. Do at least five of them this week.

5. Take a piece of paper and draw a line down the center. On one side, write down five unhelpful beliefs that seem stuck. On the other side, write the opposite of those beliefs. Say them out loud. What do they feel like in the Body?

And finally, listen to and let yourself be guided by the meditation for this chapter at thekevingarcia.com/bloommeditations.

A note on guided meditation and self-care:

Sometimes in this work, like guided meditations and somatic work, some practices can feel incredibly triggering and emotional for folks. This is your reminder that you are your own spiritual authority. Your Body knows what they are ready for, and if you become too overwhelmed at any moment, I invite you to stop, take three deep breaths, and open your eyes.

This work is slow, and it might mean you need to just journal through this stuff. It might mean you set it down and come back at another time. You're not asked to judge your reactions to these practices but to use them. Notice what happens within you and respond accordingly.

2 | LAY YOUR ASS DOWN
On Rest, Imagination, and Gentleness

You keep asking why your work is not enough, and I
don't know how to answer that, because it is enough to
exist in the world and marvel at it.
　　　　—Becky Chambers, *A Psalm for the Wild Built*

I'm a Scorpio and an enneagram 8. Suffice it to say that I am a fairly
intense person. When healthy, I'm intensely loving. When unhealthy,
I'm intensely working for an end goal without considering what is
happening on the journey there. My natural intensity also means
that staying in one place, seeking ease for myself, and knowing how
I feel are not in my wheelhouse naturally. And if there's anything my
ego scoffs at more, it's the idea of "being gentle with myself."

People said that a lot to me at the outset of my spiritual
journey and deconstruction. "Be gentle. This is a long road!"
"Be easy with yourself. You're doing your best." Ugh! Annoying.

No time for suffering here. Let me just get over it and move
on. Let me feel the thing, fix the problem, and get back to the
good vibes. They don't tell you at first that being gentle with
yourself really hurts if you've been emotionally repressed your
whole life. They don't tell you it takes time to let that shit move
through you. They don't even tell you how to do it, either! They
just say, "Be gentle. Stay soft. Keep breathing."

But I don't know how to do that. I've never been soft with myself. I've never given myself a break because I don't deserve it. I've never given myself more time or grace or any of that. I don't know how.

We've said it before: words do not teach. Experience does. No one can explain what it is to be gentle with yourself because your Gentleness is merely your natural state. Gentleness becomes the default setting when you have begun to do your work, slow down, and choose Rest over your stresses.

We find Gentleness through Rest. Rested bodies and minds. Rested hearts and souls that have a spacious and expansive place within us to move. We find Gentleness through imaging a world different than the capitalist empires that demand so much of us. And as we spend more time at ease, more time in Peace, more time practicing the things that cause us to stay in this connected space, the easier it is to let the shackles of our pain fall away. We've been fooled into thinking we don't know how to rest. Our brains have been traumatized into believing we don't have the skills needed to rest properly. We are tricked into feeling guilty anytime we find some kind of ease or reprieve from the harsh world.

Rest holds the key to you being free from these things. And the first step is realizing that you are a Divine human here to create for sheer pleasure, not a capitalist machine here to make for mere profit.

YOU ARE NOT A MACHINE

Everything I know about Rest I know from following the example and words of Tricia Hersey, the Nap Bishop and founder of The Nap Ministry. She was an exhausted seminary student, mother, poet, and artist interested in exploring ways to help herself feel better, culminating in curated spaces for sacred Rest, for napping together. She now advocates for folks to divest from the capitalist systems by laying down and following the rest path as a blueprint for resistance.

I draw from her manifesto, *Rest Is Resistance*, heavily in my conceptions of Rest as a means of liberation and a principle in my practice, a seed that bears the fruit of Gentleness. In fact, I'd say that her words are perfect and you should go read her work immediately and do what she says.

She lays out in her book how Western capitalism has bamboozled all of us into believing the lie that our productivity will be our salvation. We think our Goodness comes from our ability to create for someone else's profit. We believe that blessings and ease are only for those who work incredibly hard, break their backs for the movement, and exhaust themselves in the name of the collective. We believe that this will make us righteous, or holy, or good. But Hersey says we have been brainwashed by this. Our bodies have been programmed by deadly, toxic ideas and systems that only want us for what we can do for them. They do not love us. And therefore, as an act of radical love, we stop. We rest. We say, "Enough of this."

We have been lied to our whole lives, being told that Rest is a privilege of those who have worked for it. It's the reason we give for why we can't rest right now.

"That sounds good for you, but I work two jobs."
"Rest sounds like some privileged shit. I've got too much going on."
"I feel guilty when I slow down or take time for myself."

"I feel bad about feeling good."

"I'm so tired, but I've got bills to pay, mouths to feed."

And yet, we cannot wait any longer. The systems of this world, capitalism and white supremacy and ablism and homophobia and transmisogyny, are all conspiring against us. They keep us from coming home to our bodies by exhausting us, teaching us to hustle, showing us how to grind, by telling the lie that we are not worthy of feeling good or at ease in this life unless we bleed for it. Social media keeps us plugged in and fixated on so much of what doesn't fuel us. Our jobs demand more from us without compensation. Our expectations as caregivers, parents, or just the myth of the "good person" make any downtime we could possibly have fade into impossibility as we neglect the soft animal of our Bodies.

But Tricia Hersey paints a different picture for us, which I'll summarize here:

Rest is our God-given right. Not a leisure or extra thing to add on. Rest is our refuge. Rest is a safe place. And no one in the modern day will tell you to slow down. No one can make you lay your ass down. No one can make you stop. You must be the one to undo the lies you were told about how your worth is tied to your exhaustion level. You have been fooled into believing the lie that your work will save you, that your job is your purpose, and that you can rest later. You have been lied to. And so realize this as well:

This is not your fault. That's another lie the systems have concocted for us. Because we are bad, worthy of condemnation, lucky to be rescued by someone else's sacrifice, so if you aren't feeling the blessing, it is your fault. You must not be working hard enough or in the right way.

But there is a better way. There is space for you to slow down. In fact, by slowing down, bit by bit, over your life, you will find what you were always looking for.

Tricia Hersey also says that our imaginations, especially the imaginations of Black folks, have been stolen. "There has been a DreamSpace theft. Our ability to dream, pause, and daydream has been replaced with the robbing of time, self-worth, self-esteem, hope, and connection to ourselves and each other." You have not been able to change your beliefs because you are so distracted. You haven't been able to do anything differently because you can't imagine anything other than what you've been doing because you're too freaking tired. And this is by design.

You go to school for twelve years as soon as you can follow orders, waking up at an ungodly hour so you can be assessed on knowledge with no discernible benefit or bearing on your passion. And then, if you're lucky, they will shoulder you with costly loans, with no idea how you'll eventually pay them back. So you better hustle and get this job, so you can spend forty-plus hours a week working for barely enough income to keep up with inflation and an economy deeply fucked up by an unequal distribution of wealth. And you work so hard that by the end of the day, you're so tired, and if you're tired, you know that you worked hard, and if you worked hard, you know that you're a good boy, a good girl. And the only thing you can do to not totally off yourself is smoke this joint, watch another episode of this show, go to sleep, and start over again.

They start when you are five or six years old, putting you in programs, and we all just say yes 'cause we think this is normal. You are trained to work hard from the jump, so you think your only birthright is to toil for a meager reward. This is not normal. This is wild and unhealthy. We must begin by recognizing the abnormality of these demands and begin the work by first naming it and then imagining what better could feel like. And we get there through Rest.

We must also recognize that Rest is not a right or leisure afforded to those who work hard. Rest is your Divine right as a created being. It has been denied to you for the profit of others, and you get to say, "No more." You get to recognize your Body for what they are: a soft animal who loves what they love.

To step into Rest, you must recognize why the hell you are so tired. You must look at your life and see the ways you are being held hostage by a system that does not love you nor care if you feel good ever again. They care that you can work and produce some kind of labor that others deem profitable. And if you can't, you are disposable.

Rest is a disruption to the pattern of moving too fast.
Rest is an intentional way of caring about how you feel.
Rest is a powerful medicine.

Literally, your Body and brain need to slow down. You, in your infinite glory, with your powerful mind, may be able to will yourself to go further, and you may even push your Body to their extreme, and if you do that enough, your Body will eventually give out. This happens in the form of injury. This occurs in the form of anxiety. This happens in the form of inexplicable chronic illnesses. This occurs in the form of burning out. This happens in the form of dread that arises every time you look at the alarm clock in the morning.

I once had a student who said, "I got sick, so it feels like a nice excuse to rest." And I countered, "Sickness is sometimes a sign that you've pushed yourself too far, and now your Body is disallowing you from moving forward." This isn't 100 percent true in every scenario, but so many of us have shit immune systems because we don't give the Body enough time to recharge to do what they need to protect us. We hustle. We grind. We work as hard as we can because if we don't . . . well, we don't know what will happen. We just know we must.

Sometimes when we lay down or slow down, like meditation, whatever we are trying to ignore inevitably bubbles up. It's uncomfortable, and we wanna move away from it. Rest is a way to sit with it and let it be dissolved into ease. You've been too tired to imagine a life without this thing. The stress. The fear. The self-doubt. You have not had the space or energy to enter your dream space, to spend time in your imagination. And now we are.

So much of this work is about expanding your imagination. It is about reigniting what Dr. Willie J. Jennings called prophetic imagination. It is to realize that God is as expansive as the ever-expanding universe. Eternal. And that's something we can't wrap our temporal minds around. Then, as we spend time in that expansive imagination within, we realize that it, too, is boundless. There are ever more depths to probe. There are endless mysteries to marvel at. Rest leads us into this imagination, both through the act of napping and getting those Zs and through things that are restful.

While you may not have the time or space to physically lay down or the cash flow to work fewer hours, there are still things you can do to find rest.

Practicing five minutes of meditation at the top of your day.
Taking one minute to breathe each hour.
Purposefully finding time away from social media.
Walking in nature without any technology.
Sitting outside and feeling the sun on your skin.
Making sure that, when you get off work, you are done working and not doing more off the clock.
Finding a creative and crafty hobby to do with your hands.
Journaling regularly, even if it's short entries.
Reading poetry and inspiring prose by great minds.

This world doesn't make it easy. So you must be vigilant. You must be uncompromising. Because there is nothing more important than you staying at your center. There's nothing more crucial than you learning that your imagination is the key to your liberation.

IMAGINATION STATION

My personal practice began quite slowly. Nothing huge, nothing elaborate. Just me, on the back porch, headphones in, guided by someone on YouTube through a fifteen-minute yoga exercise. Then sitting for just a few minutes. Not praying, but breathing. And then I'd get in my car, pull up to my job at the restaurant, take a massive rip of my joint, and manage my way through the eight-hour shift, where I'd make $60. Followed by going home, feeling too exhausted to do anything else, showering, sleeping, and starting over the next day.

But I was intent on sticking to this thing that made me feel good. I recognized that there wasn't much out there that made me feel as good as tending to my physical practice. And through my own slowness, through the small moments of Peace I was finding, I realized that I was creating the feeling of Peace within me. I was the Source. And it took only a little focus.

While being broke as a joke at a shit job that overworked and underpaid me, while sharing a room in a dinky two-bedroom apartment with three people, and while navigating life as a newly out queer person who lost my entire career in the Christian nonprofit church world . . . All of that. I was still able to find some Peace. I realized this was nothing short of powerful.

Growing up in a world that taught me to hustle and a church that told me that I had to give everything to God, I was finally seeing a different way of being that felt good. I realized all the ways I was told it had to be. Even in this seemingly desperate place, I found a Peace that passed understanding. And it was me. It wasn't like God came down in a cloud or burning bush or sent an angel to say, "Babe, it's cool if you just breathe and rest and chill for a minute . . . " I realized that I was dying slowly. And I wanted to live again.

As I began leaning into Rest as a practice, especially as I was journeying through seminary, I started dreaming a lot more. My Body would be still, my breathing would be steady, and I felt like I would drop below the surface of my mind, past the choppy waters of my daily thoughts, into a place altogether easy. It felt like being wrapped in warm ocean water. I was enveloped in softness and ease. And in that space, as I stopped clinging to everything I was worried about, I luxuriated in ideas that had never come to me. I got in touch with my ancestors and those who had died before me. I saw solutions to problems I had been wondering about.

It starts so slowly. And in reality, this way of being in the world still begs me to move slower. Tricia Hersey says, "Rest is a meticulous love practice, and we will be unraveling from our sleep deprivation and socialization around rest for the remainder of our days. This is a blessing. Rest is radical because it disrupts the lie that we are not doing enough." We are learning to recognize the lies, but when they're all you've heard and all you've believed, it feels difficult to let go. It feels difficult to change our minds. But don't worry. It will happen. Your mind will shift. But it is not an overnight fix. It is not a trend you can jump on. It is not a technique you can employ once, a few times, or even periodically to ensure you don't burn out again.

It is a lifestyle shift.
It is a change of mind.
It is an active choice to resist the dominant culture.

Rest connects us back to our inner world. It is an abundant, endless source of power. It's a healing balm. If you haven't already done the meditation from the first chapter, go back and do it right now. Because my words alone cannot teach you. Words do not teach at all. Experience is the only thing that will convince you of the validity of these claims. You touching Source, slowing down enough to feel Love float to the surface of your mind as you let your rushing mind calm. There is nothing I can do to even give you a glimpse. You must choose this for yourself.

On a physiological level, sleep allows the Body and mind time to naturally repair and regenerate. The mind gets to sort through the data and thoughts rushing around. If the idea of slowing down to access Rest feels like an impossible task, this is the sign that you can't delay a moment longer in your fight for your Body's well-being. It is a sign that you are currently brainwashed. It is a sign that you are a captive. And Rest, my love, this is rebellion.

If you are trying to save the entire world yet cannot save yourself, what hope do you have to accomplish it? The world will not be saved by exhausted bodies and souls. All will be made new by people with the energy and stamina to see our work through to the end. The worst part is, this will not be accomplished in our lifetimes. We are firming the foundation set for us by those who came before us.

Again, Rest isn't just napping. It is meditation. It is looking out the window at your nine-to-five. It is daydreaming. It is resting your eyes on the hour and letting the good feelings that are being held down below your anxieties rise to the surface. Rest is walking in nature. Rest is reading a book on something inspiring, finding poetry that lights you up, and being with people who don't demand anything but that you be yourself.

Imagine that. Being yourself . . . what might that be like?

A SENSE OF LEISURE IS ESSENTIAL

The last line of the first lesson in ACIM's workbook for students is, "A comfortable sense of leisure is essential." This is so crucial. At first, the rote practice of showing up and doing the thing feels robotic or forced because, in some ways, it is. You are disrupting your patterns, actions, and thoughts, which have led you to your suffering. As you move through the practices and begin to understand the effects, as you see what it gives you, a sense of leisure arises. A sense of "I want to do this for the Joy of it, for the feeling of it, for the thrill of it."

I keep this practice because of the pleasure it brings me. And that may seem base or selfish, but we must realize and accept that we're all doing this. We are all doing things because we think they are going to make us feel good. We do things because we believe on some level that it will get us closer to what we want. And as for me, I want to feel ease. I want to feel a sense of buoyancy. I want to feel good. And my spiritual practice should follow suit. It should help me feel easy, good. I want it to feel like a leisure activity, an indulgence even. Instead of a task I must complete to be holy, it is a practice I keep to remind me that I am holy.

Leisure is defined as the use of free time for enjoyment. Beloved, your practice is to be enjoyable. If you find it challenging to step back from how you've always done things, remember that you're not in a rush. There is no hurry, for you are going on a journey that is already complete. You're looking for the Peace that exists inside you. Because stressing over the reality that you are not resting . . . kinda defeats the purpose.

When I first came out, I was still in hustle mode. I had all the trappings of an early content creator and blogger who wanted to be famous, to make money doing what I loved while also trying to do advocacy work in Christian spaces. My work schedule was 9:00 a.m. to 5:00 p.m. and then 6:00 p.m. to 11:30 p.m. working on other things. And I was so mad while I did it.

It was so irritating to me that mediocre white, cishet, Christian dudes could create platforms and share stuff with so little substance and zero integrity, and people ate that bullshit up. It was infuriating to work so hard for so little recognition and return. And I felt so righteous in it. Hard work should yield the rewards, right? That's what capitalism taught me.

But that's not how it works for queer people. I could never ultimately be myself in those spaces and be fully loved. And yet I worked as hard as I could to get their approval. I tried to show what a good and faithful person I was and declare to them that I belonged at the table of Christ just as much as they did.

I grew tired. I grew resentful. And I was mad because the revolution I craved wasn't happening fast enough. The reformation I dreamed of, the revival I saw in my mind's eye, was nowhere in physical sight. And for some reason, I thought that was my fault too. I worked my ass off and nothing was changing. On top of that, I was doing all the right things, I was being a good little progressive person, a good little liberal Christian, and I still didn't feel any better. I was working hard to be one of the good guys, and yet I still didn't feel good.

I was growing disillusioned with life. I lacked purpose. All I knew was I just had to keep going. And I did it until I burnt out. I did exactly what I was programmed to do, exactly what I did before, just focusing my energy in a different direction. Granted, it was a better direction, but it still didn't give me what I wanted. And what was it that I really wanted?

To finally just feel baseline okay. To just take a breath without worry choking me. To not worry if God was gonna send me to hell. To be happy . . . and it was clear that this was not giving me what I wanted.

We have to recognize what we really want. Then we need to recognize *what gives us* the thing we want and stop settling for shit that underdelivers. Hustling, pushing, grind culture, all of these are distractions from the real prize and the true path. We must recognize that feeling better will not come from sheer force of will but a willingness to stop doing what is so freaking hard, what is contrary to our actual nature.

Cultivating a spiritual practice is a lot like getting a garden ready. If the garden hasn't been attended to, there are vines and weeds and overgrowth to remove first. If the soil is tough, it must be tilled before a seed will take root.

So, believe me, I get that this shit feels hard. It seems impossible to make space. It feels almost shameful to declare that Rest is your birthright. But everything feels hard the first time you do it.

Rather than thinking you have to totally change your life today, that you must shift your lifestyle drastically and immediately, why not just give it a rest? Let the thought that tells you this is hard go. Let the idea that this is going to take forever before you feel better go. Let the inner critic saying that you must work for this go. Let it all go. Just focus on right now. What would make you feel good?

Rest is that gateway to seeing that there is a different way of being. Just from the mere act of laying your ass down for a time, you will find that the stresses that keep you up at night haunt you a little less and then, in time, stop haunting you altogether. You will see the urgency that you've been conditioned to respond to is an illusion. And you'll begin to ask, "What would make me feel good?"

With as much ease as possible, move toward that, knowing it doesn't need to be perfect for you to continue. It has to be consistent. You must choose yourself over and over again. You must decide to lay down again and again. Choose to rest again and again because in this particular timeline, in a lifetime where we will not see an end to capitalism's lies and systems, we must "snatch our rest" back from the hands of the false God.

And as you rest, see what it does for you. Wonder about it. Be curious about it. Notice how it makes you feel. Notice how easy it was to give yourself some time to breathe. An hour's siesta in the middle of the day. A thirty-minute power nap. Fifteen minutes of focused breathing. Ten minutes of staring out a window to watch the leaves with incredible intention. Eight minutes of repeating a mantra. Five minutes of listening to a guided meditation. One minute of mindful breathing.

This work is about deprogramming from the violence that the system demands of your Body. To work yourself beyond your limitations at a machine level for so little pay that you have just enough brain space to worry about how the hell you're going to get up and do it the next day is violence. And that is not normal. Tricia Hersey says it repeatedly: we have been bamboozled by the lies of the capitalist empire. We work so hard for so little because we believe we are only as much as we produce.

Committing to rest is a commitment to "a lifelong, consistent, meticulous love practice." It is choosing, in every way that you can, to totally let go of the lie that you are not enough, that you don't deserve to feel good, that you must work to the point of exhaustion to prove you are worthy, that you are a machine, that you must do something brilliant to be lovable.

And as you move more and more into this idea that your Peace and ease are your default, you won't have to try and be gentle with yourself. You will be in touch with your natural state of Gentleness.

NOT DIFFICULT. DIFFERENT.

When you are self-controlled, your actions are naturally gentle. Gentleness is not something you have to work for. Being gentle takes the same amount of effort as being shitty to yourself, but the results are much better. We think that if we shame ourselves enough, if we verbally abuse ourselves and keep ourselves from doing the things that will make us feel better, we will somehow achieve salvation. We'll somehow become peaceful the more we go to war with ourselves. We cut ourselves off from Source to prove we are worthy of the Source we claim we want to be with so badly, when the reality is, we could just let go a bit, close our eyes, and breathe.

We could just as quickly see Peace as we can see all the fearful imaginations in our heads. The only difference between the Peace you want to feel and where you presently are is a matter of focus.

It takes enormous brainpower to change our mind patterns because we've practiced a shitty one for so long. But stop saying that this shit is hard.

This is not hard.

Breathing is not hard. You do it all the time. You just don't pay attention. You are thinking all the time, but you just don't pay attention.

Anytime you find yourself saying, "This is hard," I want you to say instead, "This is not difficult. It is different." And it is. Being gentle with yourself is different than the punishment system we have set up. It is an antithesis to the sacrificial model of love set up for us. It is ease and expanse. It gives you every-thing you want and need and illuminates a path ahead, and you are gentle with the moments when you aren't there yet. You realize you're looking for your path of least resistance instead of the one littered with glass, rocks, and pain.

When you realize what the practice gives you, a way to be self-controlled in the sweetness of Gentleness, you become more than willing to return to it. You must realize what this is giving you. Notice, on the days when you keep a practice, how do you feel? When you're stressed, ask, "Did I meditate today?" Notice the difference in the quality of your life when you give yourself just a bit of time at the top of the day versus just raw-dogging life without preparing your mind and Body to resist the program-ming of the world.

No one is asking for perfection here. I'm just telling you, be easy about this. There's no destination because you're already home. There's no completing this thing because you'll never get it done. But you didn't come here to get it done. You came here to create it, enjoy it, love it, and then create some more.

Come home to your Self first, and then worry about the Rest. Commit to your Body feeling good, get yourself in a consis-tent rhythm of keeping yourself there, maintaining it, and then watch how clarity comes in.

And by the time you make this a priority, you will realize that Gentleness is no longer something you have to strive for.

THE SOFT ANIMAL OF YOUR BODY

You've heard me say, "the soft animal of your Body" a few times so far. I draw a line from the famous Mary Oliver poem "Wild

Geese." If you ever need a holy text on Gentleness, this is the one. In it, she gives the greatest advice on how to love yourself through all of this. "You only have to let the soft animal of your body / love what it loves."

Your Body isn't a machine. Your Body is a soft animal, and you are their steward. You have been taught to make your Body your subject, to push them beyond their capabilities, to be all mind over matter, not realizing it doesn't matter without a right mind. If you can begin to treat your Body, the soft animal of your Body, with tenderness, as one who needs the most compassion, your healing journey will be so much easier.

This poem is the best way I know how to sum up and describe Gentleness as a quality. To let the soft animal of your Body just love what it loves, to let them be whatever they are, and to love them for the sake of the pleasure of it, that is Gentleness.

It breaks my heart that we have such trouble loving ourselves these days. We willingly put on a crown of thorns, take on these harsh and untrue thought patterns, unable to access the loving thoughts God has for us, and do it because we think it makes us good. But you are already good. And you don't need to repent for anything except the idea that you are separate from love, unworthy of feeling good, and don't deserve Rest.

When you actively make your Rest part of your practice, knowing it leads you back to life, knowing that Gentleness feels way better than self-condemnation, you become something deliciously different. You become a creature with determination and a clear vision of what you could create.

Through your own Gentleness, you become willing. And even the slightest bit of willingness can change everything.

MANTRAS FOR LAYING YOUR ASS DOWN

I am enough now.
If I am tired, I'm going to lay down.
I am worthy of feeling good.
I find spaces in my day to return to a restful state.
This rest is my birthright.

THINGS TO THINK ABOUT:

◆ What is my relationship to Rest right now? A reality or an impossibility? Somewhere in between?

◆ What stories do I tell myself about Rest? About people who Rest? About leisure and ease?

◆ How do I want to change my thinking and inner programming around productivity and purpose?

THINGS TO TRY:

1. Take a nap. For real, go lay your ass down and set a timer for ten to fifteen minutes. Don't get up. Close your eyes. Be easy. Go for thirty minutes if you have the time.

2. Look at your daily schedule and commit to a time to recenter. It could be one-minute meditations on the hour or a few minutes before and after work to move you back to Peace. Just find the time. Be uncompromising in this.

3. Spend twenty minutes sitting on the couch, looking at the leaves on the trees outside. If it's warm, go out and sky-gaze for twenty minutes.

4. Attend a sound bath or other immersive artistic healing experience. Or find a yin yoga or other restorative, easy yoga class. Or attend a meditation workshop with others. Do something with people that would make you feel so good.

5. Plan regular sabbaths from social media, work, and technology, and keep them. This could look like two hours a week for you and your journal. This could look like setting your phone down at a specific time and not picking it up till later.

And listen to the immersive meditation on Rest available at thekevingarcia.com/bloommeditations.

3 | 1 PERCENT

On Willingness, Devotion, and Faithfulness

I heard a voice inside my head. It disagreed.
And if it wasn't God, then thank God it was me.
—Maddie Zahm, *If It's Not God*

Picture it: Tennessee. 1999. I'm roughly nine years of age, going on ten. I had just spent the week at a place called Camp Christian, where all the middle school youth group kids ended up for one week each summer. It holds fond memories for me. I felt like I belonged there. I was still young and held what I now know was innocence. And it was at that camp that I walked down the aisle at the altar call and confessed my belief and need for Jesus Christ to be my personal savior.

When I tell people that I was a pious little kid, this is what I mean. I mean I met Jesus at age nine and was fully sold out for the kingdom. But looking back on it now, I really think I had a mystical encounter with Christ. It was a moment when I had such perfect clarity about what Love really was. How much God loved me felt so clear and so evident. I remember I wanted to get baptized with everyone else, and my mother had to be called, and she said she wanted me to wait until I got back home to do it at our church.

I felt off about this. I didn't understand. I had already made my declaration of faith. What is to stop me from being baptized? I wanted to be baptized here, where I felt fully alive. I wanted to seal that moment.

Weeks later, I was sitting across from the youth pastor at our church who I didn't know at all, but even at nine years old, I found him quite attractive. He asked me, "Why do you wanna get baptized?" I answered something about going to heaven and feeling called to follow Jesus, wanting my sins forgiven, and feeling this deep Love of God. I just knew this was the right thing to do.

He told me, "Yeah, it's all those things, but the main thing is, you gotta be willing to be lead, willing to be taught. That's what it means to be a disciple." And I did. I was young, but I was not dumb. I felt this conviction, and I was ready. A few weeks later, on July 4, 1999, upon my confession of faith before the congregation, I was baptized as a brother in the name of the Father, the Son, and the Holy Spirit. I went under, I came up, and I felt . . . nothing.

I was confused. What was all that amazing energy I felt at camp when I was dancing around the woods under the moon? Where was it now? Did I do it wrong? I prayed that the Holy Spirit would show me how to bring that feeling back, what I thought was the presence of God. I didn't wanna be outside of it. After I changed out of my wet clothes, my family went to a Mexican restaurant to eat chimichangas, which was customary for us on Sundays.

I grew in age and in faith. I read my Bible voraciously, letting its words become a part of my soul, while most of my friends complained that their quiet times (that's the evangelical version of a devotional practice where you pray and read your Bible) were so bland and boring. The words they read were stale, and they felt like God didn't really hear them. But as for me, I'm one of those weirdos for whom quiet time was enjoyable. No one forced me to do these things.

In my teen years, I became very interested in issues of justice thanks to Shane Claiborne's *Irresistible Revolution* and *Jesus for President*. I continued to be faithful to the church because I thought that I could not love Christ and hate his bride. I thought they were a package deal, and I was also convinced that the church was the best mechanism for helping create real, lasting change in the world. And, of course, we were doing the work: saving souls. As long as we were focused on saving the soul of the person in front of us, poor behavior was seen as righteousness. As long as I could deprive myself of the things that I truly wanted, I could look at others with an air of superiority. If I could do it, why can't you?

I made myself follow a path of self-negation through ex-gay therapy and ministries, trying to "fix" my sexuality by becoming straight. And I thought that my feelings of constant suffering, the pain I endured for my Faithfulness, would eventually be rewarded. And if not in this life, then in heaven! We were often reminded that this life was a blink in the grand scheme of eternity. But that prospect was horrifying to me.

How could this comfort me? The idea that being alone for the rest of my life because I couldn't overcome my "sexual issues" would be okay because I'd never be alone in heaven? Y'all want me to just live my life feeling miserable for an indeterminant amount of time? Gotta say, not a great offer.

After years and years of living faithfully into my celibacy, into making myself small, I just could not take it anymore. One night at the men's group I was attending, the leader of my group was sharing this sentiment, and rather than just bowing to his Wisdom and eldership, I told him to go fuck himself because how the hell does that help me now? How does salvation later do anything to alleviate the pain I'm in now? A theological platitude like that is a nice cross-shaped Band-Aid on a gaping spiritual wound.

I was faithful to this version of a white, straight, male Jesus, to this church that told me that the only way to belong was to resist the possibility of ever experiencing romance or deep, intimate pleasure, and not just the sexual kind but the ability to be fully known at all.

I was faithful, and I was so lonely.
I was faithful, and I was in so much pain.
I was faithful, and it never felt like it was enough.
I was faithful, and I gave my everything.
I was faithful, played the game, and did it perfectly.
I was faithful.

And I still lost everything.
And what was I faithful to?

I was faithful to a way of being that exhausted me. I was faithful to a lie. I was faithful to people and institutions that were not faithful to me, people who claimed unconditional Love for me, and places that said everyone belongs, which was a lie. I found the edge. I found the boundary. And it turns out, I was always outside of it.

Faithfulness, you've maybe been taught, looks like devotion without question. It seems like following rules. It sounds like yes sir and no ma'am. It feels like a comfortable chair until you drink the little deconstruction potion, and like Alice, you grow, the chair breaks, and you're stuck. Faithfulness, as we have learned it, is nothing short of consenting to your abuse.

And now here we are, better than being stuck where we were but nowhere near where we wanna be because we're still faithful to things that aren't faithful to us. We are faithful to our jobs, which give us the most stress and usually not enough compensation because we are afraid we will not be able to make rent. We are faithful to people who gaslight us and make us feel terrible because we are scared of being alone. We are faithful to everything. Everything except what makes us bloom.

We have been fooled, once again, into believing that suffering and Love are somehow connected to one another. Evangelical Christianity has programmed into us the idea that suffering is the path to salvation and that if you aren't sacrificing in some way, you're not truly devoted.

A Course in Miracles tells us, "You who believe that sacrifice is Love must learn that sacrifice is separation from Love. For sacrifice brings guilt as surely as Love brings Peace. Guilt is the condition of sacrifice, as Peace is the condition for the awareness of your relationship with God."

Give up your obsession with being good enough and open yourself to the reality that you are Good. And you might roll your eyes again. You might say, "It's not that easy." But isn't it? I'm not saying you have to believe it. I'm saying be open to it. You are Good with a capital G.

And there's already a part of you that believes that.

AT LEAST 1 PERCENT

There's a saying that my friends in recovery circles have shared with me. "Are you willing to take at least 1 percent of the responsibility for your sobriety?" Hearing that statement shifted something in me. I think, for so much of my life, I had felt like I had no control. I was powerless before a mean God figure, and no matter what I tried, things never worked out how I thought they should. I thought I was the problem, not considering the system I was working within was flawed and not built for someone like me to flourish.

So many of those who are stuck in unhealthy Christian spaces and high-pressure religious communities are measured against a rubric of perfection they could never hope to aspire to. And these communities teach us to be codependent on them. They trick us into surrendering our power and our authority to them. And so when we escape, we are so spiritually and mentally atrophied that it results in arrested development.

We get stuck in the pain. And now that we are finally focusing on it, we fixate on it because what else are we supposed to do? It's almost like a prophecy fulfilled itself: We were told that if we left, we would be miserable. We were told that, outside of our church communities, there was weeping and gnashing of teeth. We were convinced that it was outside of God's will. And here we are, not stuck in those places but still feeling just as miserable.

And, on top of all that, we are completely unaware that another way is possible. Sometimes we're even resistant to finding a new way because we think, What if this fails me too? What happens when this ultimately disappoints me too? And onward and so on. The mind gives us all the reasons to stay where we are because we aren't sure that we could survive if we move on from our spiritual crash zones. What if it gets worse?

Beloved, this is where I ask for your trust. This is where I ask you a similar question. Are you willing to take at least 1 percent of the responsibility for your own spiritual recovery? For your own happiness? For your own Joy? Is there even the smallest part of you that wants to feel better? Can you focus on that little bit and see how it grows?

My friend and former student, Chelsea, is an incredible person. She's been sober for nearly a decade, and one of the ways she lights up is when she's helping other people on their recovery path. She introduced me to the brilliant concepts from twelve-step programs around a person's individual responsibility to keep themselves sober.

She told me this story: A person came into their AA meeting one night, introduced themselves, and sobbed. "I don't know how to stop!" Just crying and crying that they were out of control and didn't know what to do. And a person with twenty years of sobriety looked them dead in the face and said, "Well, if you can't stop, then don't stop. Go. Go to the bar and get drunk."

The person crying stopped, confused at this advice. "It's not that you don't know how to. We all know how to. Don't put alcohol in your system. You have to be willing to do something else. So if you aren't willing to do something else, keep doing what you're doing. See how you'll end up." To my knowledge, that person kept coming and is still sober to this day.

This may seem a little antithetical to the soft edge of 1 percent that I was painting. And maybe that's what you need, a soft edge and easy invitation back into Love. But for others, the longer you've been bitter, the longer you've been stewing in your pain or resentment or feelings of separation, the harder it feels to begin something new. Your Body is holding fast to walls of self-protection. This work, however, is learning how to let go of your defenses and just let Love in.

Are you willing? Are you willing to try something else? Then, my love, do the thing. Do the smallest thing to get closer to Peace.

There comes a part very early in our spiritual practice where we will get a taste of the good feelings, we'll see a benefit from our daily ritual, and then something interrupts us. Something gets in the way of us keeping our practice.

Are you willing to take at least 1 percent of the responsibility for your spiritual recovery? Are you willing to do the bare minimum to help ground yourself in your Body, to still your mind? Is there at least 1 percent of you that wants to feel better? And what is that 1 percent today?

For some, this feels so easy. And for others, this feels like the most weighty and intense thing you've ever attempted. It feels terrifying. But don't worry, babe. I've got you. And as a reminder, this is slow work. But you must, must, must make the first move.

Another thing I borrow from my friends in recovery circles is really taking it one day at a time. They say it is easier to focus on just staying sober today and not to think about staying sober tomorrow or for the rest of your life. It's the same thing with spiritual practice and your spiritual sobriety. You don't need to worry about a big lifestyle change. You need to take it one day at a time. What does it look like to come back to Peace in the present moment? To feel it in your Body here and now?

How many of us have the grand vision of changing our lives and then never, in not a single way, do the things we claim we want to do? I'm writing this on January 2, 2023. The number of people on my social media timeline declaring that they will change their whole life, working out, meditating, manifesting, clean eating, losing weight, whatever . . . we all know is not helpful. Still, we feel this pressure every January to be better than we are, as if what we are right now isn't enough. Not to mention that overhauling our lives in January doesn't really harmonize with the seasons. It's winter in the northern hemisphere, and all our animal cousins have been napping for the most part. What have we been doing? Pushing to get the last bit of things done before the end of the year, only to go harder as soon as the ball drops at midnight. If anything, the back and beginning of the year should be marked by doing less.

Capitalism and grind culture, and yes, the church, have taught us an unhealthy imbalance approach to life. We think we must be all in on everything all the time. We gotta be sold out for something, some cause outside of the pleasure and creativity of these bodies. But believe me when I tell you that consistent, simple practices will serve you more than trying to shift your life-style in one swoop.

Rather than thinking that you must start your hour-long meditation practice today and reach enlightenment by six weeks in or else, imagine a one-minute approach where you just focus on what it feels like to breathe. Imagine telling yourself for two minutes, "I love my Body." Imagine looking at yourself every day in the mirror, naked, and saying, "You are so beautiful." Imagine taking a walk and pretending to have never seen anything before. What Wonder might you feel?

I'm advocating for you to do just a little at first. One minute. A small mantra you repeat to counter your bullshit programming. I'm asking for 1 percent willingness. Is there any part of you that wants to be well? That wants to be done with this bullshit way of life that isn't working for you? Is there 1 percent of you that wants to be truly happy?

You might not be practiced in leaning into this side of yourself yet. And that's normal. Again, things feel challenging when you do them for the first time. But is it an insurmountable challenge? No, of course not. It's different. And it feels unfamiliar. But doesn't it feel better?

As you are willing to keep your practice, even imperfectly, you can expect more and more that you will feel grounded and in Love. And as your practice gives you what you want and leads you into Peace consistently, you'll notice that it's not that you just like doing it but that it becomes hard to live without it.

SWEETNESS

When I work with people, I teach them meditative practices and help walk them through their personal blocks. The thing I love hearing a few weeks into working together is, "I didn't do my practice today, and I noticed the difference." It's so subtle; once you know how good you can feel, it feels wrong to deny yourself that. And it feels wrong not because skipping your practice makes you a "bad" person but because suddenly not taking care of yourself is not in line with who You are. And your Body is now telling you, louder and louder each time, through your emotions and intuition, which way to go, which thoughts to follow, and what action to take. There is, for me and others as well, a kind of sweetness that comes with the practice. The feeling of ease, the sensation of being at home in the Body, and the sense of deep Love are so yummy to me. Again, I can't describe it to you.

It comes in silence. It comes in recognition of Love's presence within. And once you taste it, you cannot live without it. In fact, you become unwilling to live below that standard of Joy.

To me, it feels akin to the concept of Bhakti Yoga. Swami Vivekananda, an Indian mystic and Hindu monk with some of the most prolific writings on yoga, describes this as the yoga of devotion. It's a particular type of yoga wherein there is an object of devotion, someone or something you venerate. There are countless paths within this, but what Vivekananda points at in his works on Bhakti is this: "Until you have that thirst, that desire, you cannot get religion, however you may struggle with your intellect, or your books, or your forms."

You have to be thirsty. You must be hungry for Love. That is the requirement. You must desire to connect with Source, and why? Because it is connecting with Life itself. Because it makes you bloom. Because it produces within you a sweetness that is better than what you were experiencing before.

But you can't get there without the willingness to do something about it.

That is what my practice gives me because of how it makes me feel. To me, nothing is sweeter than finding my place in heaven, nothing more amazing than realizing that it's right here. Nothing is more wonderful than letting go of things that aren't helpful anymore. There is nothing more perfect than this breath. That is what I am devoted to.

With consistency and earnestness in practice, willingness becomes devotion, the conscious loyalty toward the thing that makes you bloom. It is moving from mere curiosity to enthusiastic commitment to something or someone because of what it brings out in you.

JESUS: BROTHER, FRIEND, AND TEACHER

I often hear something similar from people who are deconstructing their faith. "I don't wanna lose Jesus." Or "I still love Jesus, but I just can't go back to church." Great news: you don't have to go back to church. But I have a question: Do you think Jesus is something to be lost?

Here's the deal with Jesus, or any metaphysical Wisdom figure for that matter: their reality, or rather your ability to prove their existence in terms of what we call time and space, doesn't matter as much as the imagination they inspire within you. You can learn all sorts of things about God and never know God. You can be a New Testament scholar and know all the gospels by heart and never hear from Jesus. You can even speak in the tongues of men and angels and not know Love.

If Jesus is a helpful person to you, if you feel a call from or a love for Jesus, you don't have to let that go if you don't want to. But if, in your mind and Body, the person of Jesus feels too triggering, threatening, or just too much, let him go. He's around if you want. Or not if you don't. Either way, I'm sure he doesn't care.

When I say I am devoted to Jesus, it is because of what Jesus brings out in me. He's no longer this far-off demigod figure with a taste for wine at weddings and punishing people for wrong beliefs. Jesus is my teacher, my brother, and my friend. Jesus reminds me of what is possible for me. Jesus shows me the path back to heaven. I concentrate on him, and I'm moved past my insecurities and ushered into the temple of my heart. There, I am reminded of what is true. Jesus grounds me. And that's why I am devoted. Not because he saved my soul from eternal damnation but because he woke me up to the reality that I am Love incarnate. That I am in heaven. That I am Wonder, fully made.

What's annoying to me is that my devotion to Jesus keeps me in proximity to people who believe they have a monopoly on him and are confident that I am the devil. I am not interested in debating this. To me, it's not essential if you believe me. I'm only doing what is making me bloom. I'm only faithful to the practices that make me come alive. I'm only trying to keep my Peace and be happy with the time I have left on this rock spinning through infinite space. And if that disturbs you, then baby, you gotta ask yourself why. If someone else is annoyed or threatened by you protecting your Peace, then it is likely they've never felt it themselves and likely cannot understand.

I'm devoted to this. And like I was devoted to the church, willing to give my time and energy and Body for the sake of this other thing flourishing at my own expense, I now am devoted to my Body. I will give what it takes to keep my Body safe, make myself feel whole, and stay aware of Love's presence. My love, that is steadfast Faithfulness.

When I was a devout Christian, my pastors and teachers would always tell us how we should be so on fire for Jesus, how our Love for him should permeate everything, that people would ask what is different about us. What gives us Joy? When I tell you I felt so awkward about telling people about this weird gospel that demanded they be something other than who they were . . . yikes.

When I was a missionary, we were in very rural Romania. I remember our task one afternoon was to walk around one area of town with our pastor, our host, and translator and witness to people. Like, go up to them and ask them if they knew the Lord.

Get them to maybe pray the sinner's prayer. But at minimum, ask if we could pray for them. We walked around all afternoon, and no one wanted to talk to us. A lot of the local kids would run past and point and laugh. The pastor informed us that we were being made fun of. "They are calling us 'repenters' because of the gospel we proclaim. But I don't mind." He laughed, and I didn't think much of it. But looking back at it now, I realize the pastor must've been infamous for this behavior of proselytizing to folks.

Anyways, during one afternoon when we were out on our "witness walks," a time when we would walk around and just tell people about Jesus and invite them to church (it was as cringe as you think), we came across two old women at a bus stop. As we started a conversation, we learned both were devout Eastern Orthodox Christians. We talked about Jesus, and they crossed themselves when we talked about our love for our savior and were so lovely. And at the same time, the pastor was insistent about giving them a gospel tract (a little pamphlet explaining how without Jesus, they were bound for hell, and more specifically, how this version of Jesus was the only real one). I can't tell you how awkward it was. It felt so fucking weird and wrong. These women had a connection to God. It was obvious. Why the hell did I need to change them? I could see they were faithful to what was keeping them connected.

It was the same story everywhere I went. The Buddhist monks I met in Myanmar. The Hindu devotees in India. They all had a connection to the eternal. Their Faithfulness was evident and effortless. In fact, I was jealous of what they had. A stillness and ease. No need to force it or make others believe what they believe for them to experience the Divine.

And also, they didn't stay in their faith because of fear of hell. They remained faithful because of what their practice did for them. They kept the faith because of what their faith produced in their lives. The same must become true for you. If there is any fear in your faith, it is not love but manipulation. If there is guilt in your practice, it is not righteousness you attain but merely reprieve from feeling wrong. But if you recognize what it gives you, and you feel the small amount of willingness it takes to turn toward what turns you on, what makes you come alive, what makes you come back into Peace, your devotion will remain steady. And devotion, with earnestness and consistency, becomes Faithfulness.

My reference point for this presence is Jesus. He's the teacher I've known the longest, and frankly, at this point in my life, I don't have the energy or desire to try and learn an entirely new faith system when there are treasures at my fingertips. If I were in Asia, I'd likely be Buddhist, Hindu, or Sikh. Were I in the Middle East, Muhammad or Bahá'u'lláh might've been my main prophet. But I was born in the South of the American Empire in the late twentieth century. And I can either be annoyed by that, which trust me, I am, or I can adapt. I can learn. I can expand anyways, despite what the dominant culture says is allowed.

What feels so dope is, suddenly, on this side of my life and deconstruction, I want to tell everyone about this. (Hence the book!) I want to say to folks that it's possible to approach their faith practice without the bullshit of patriarchy and pain. It is possible to feel deep Love without having to sacrifice anything. In fact, the only way to feel the Love you want is to find the things that will help you feel pleasure and Joy. I'm faithful to this practice because it makes me come alive, and the way that I find I can expand this Joy, this creative energy, this good feeling, is by giving it away.

Now that I keep my practices, now that I am at Peace and ease, and now that I'm connected to Source, I can finally give in the way that I want to, in a generative way. I can begin to stand in true solidarity with people instead of just serving for the sake of paying for my sins.

Just 1 percent, babe. Are you willing to take 1 percent of the responsibility for your spiritual recovery? Focus on that 1 percent. Give your attention to it and see how your energy grows in that, as you will see what joyful things you step into.

MANTRAS FOR FINDING WILLINGNESS

I am more than willing to take 1 percent of the responsibility for my healing.
I am willing to keep my commitment to my spiritual practice.
I am willing to be wrong.
I am willing to receive help.

THINGS TO THINK ABOUT:

♦ What has been my hang-up or obstacle to sustaining my practices? Have I been willing before?

♦ What am I presently devoted to? (Hint: it's what you do with your time.) What is my devotion doing for me?

♦ What would it be like to be faithful to my Body? To be devoted to my connection with my Self?

THINGS TO TRY:

1. When you realize you've forgotten to do your practice, ask yourself in the moment, "Am I willing to do it now? Can I do it now?" If it's yes and yes, stop, even for a minute, and find your center. If you can't in the moment, commit to a moment later in your day where you center yourself.

2. Write down the things you used to do out of a sense of guilt or obligation. What did those feel like? Conversely, write down at least three things you know feel really good and grounding. Why do these feel good?

3. Do at least one of the good things listed in number 2.

4. Think of someone faithful to their cause, practice, friends, or family. What do they do?

5. As way of keeping track of your practice, set a reminder in your phone for the middle of your day with the question, "Did you practice today?" If yes, dismiss the notification. If not, are you willing to take one minute to breathe and remember what Peace feels like? If not now, will you commit to another time in your day?

And listen to the immersive meditation on Faithfulness at thekevingarcia.com/bloommeditations.

4 | FORGET FINDING COMMUNITY

On Friendship, Solidarity, and Generosity

Any time your empathy, your solidarity, is with the little people, you're with the cross. If you identify with the lynchers, then, no, you can't understand what's happening.

—James Cone, *The Cross and the Lynching Tree*

Were you the volunteer of the year at your church? And by that I mean, were you the person they could call if they needed something, anything? And you loved doing it because people told you how thankful they were for you, what a blessing you were to the church or community? Does that or did that extend to your family? Are you the person to not eat until everyone else is totally done? Are you the person who ensures everyone else is good before they even begin to try and become okay? Have you ever said, "I serve people. That's how I find my purpose."?

I will agree that service is an indisputable pathway toward self-realization. Selfless service is a beautiful virtue. But too few people truly understand the selfless part. Too many understand how to manipulate willing hands who are grasping for validation of their own Goodness. (Aka, they know how to get people to do free labor.) Too many of us got our purpose from serving the church, and now that we have nothing to do with our time, we feel useless. We're not laboring in some way, and we feel bad for it.

Knowing now how capitalism has informed so much of our spiritual lives, it probably comes as no surprise at this point that our view of service and generosity is also kinda fucked up. Because, once again, we've been taught that sacrifice is necessary to receive Love. We learn to ignore the Body and the suffering we experience because suffering is part of the game. And this is no clearer than when we brutalize ourselves for the sake of our local church.

My mom was the worship leader at our church. It was a completely volunteer gig, like everyone (minus the pastor's job). And she was really good at it, even though she wasn't a trained musician. She also was the one to put together the annual children's Christmas musical, dressing between thirty and fifty kids up in costumes, teaching them all the songs and motions, directing their little acting hearts, and bringing the whole community together. This was on top of raising her kids and a bunch of other kids as a full-time daycare worker. And she was also the one who transformed all the classrooms of the church into various adventure zones during the VBS each summer. Like . . . even though it was low-key indoctrination, my mother's devotion to the church was beautiful. She did it because she loved seeing folks come alive, especially kids. She loved how parents saw their kids blossom.

As lovely as that was, I think I learned how to over-function in the church from her. Even as we moved away from that church I grew up in, she did the most; as a result, her kids also did the most. We were all going all the time, giving all the time, and that was the culture. By all standards of what we were given, we were doing it "right." However, even when you're doing it right, it is never enough for a hungry white male god who needs sacrifice.

There's this old song by Relient K, a very popular band with youth group kids across the US during the late 90s and early 2000s. It's from one of the earlier albums, and I wish I could go shake Matthew Thiessen, the writer, and say, "BABE, STOP."

The chorus says, "I'll give, give, give / until there's nothing else. / Give my all, until it all runs out." If that's not indicative of the pressure we were all feeling and the behavior that we venerated at the time, I don't know what would be. But I lived into that.

I gave my all, cash included. I was a tither. I was also the person who gave on top of my tithes. I was also the person who volunteered my time for a lot of stuff. On any given weekend, I was working ten to fifteen hours for setup, rehearsal, worship service, and teardown, as well as driving an hour to the next city over to do another service at our church's other campus. I volunteered with the youth group on Wednesdays, setting up, doing the actual worship set, sitting through the sermon, tearing down, serving on the prayer team, and whatever they needed. I was a full-time music student and campus leader at my university. And this was the mantra: *Give until there's nothing left.* That's what God deserves. Everything from me.

And we call this performative exhaustion "generosity."

We have been taught that generosity is whether or not we fulfill these seemingly compulsory requests for our labor and resources. Good people are generous people, we are told. We give because we think it's the right thing to do. Even those who have deconstructed still over-function out of a toxic sense of service. This again leaves us in the grip of sacrifice. We give and give until there is nothing left in the name of "community," never seeing ourselves as worthy of the healing we claim to advocate for others.

Beloved, you can't lead somewhere you've never been. You cannot give someone things you do not possess. You wanna make the world more peaceful? You find the Peace in your Self first. You want the world to be more equitable? Find equanimity in your breath. And see how much more capable you are.

So many of us have developed a warped sense of community. We thought we were to be lost within the whole. We thought we had to surrender our identity, differences, and what makes us unique, creative souls to keep this institution alive. And they call that institution a "community" or a "church family." They breed loyalty and devotion in us, which in time becomes codependence on the group's approval. Then you deconstructed and left, yet you still find yourself desperate for that sense of belonging.

According to fascinating research done by one of my fellow internet humans, Brandon Flannery, the thing most deconstructing people of faith miss is community. They miss having people to mark seasons with, to participate in weekly activities with, and individuals to lean on in hard times. But I think it's simpler than that. I think we are lonely because we have no friends now. I think we aren't craving "community" as much as we are craving deep, intimate, holy relationships that fill us up. We believe that having something like what we had before, a group of folks with similar beliefs who like to sing songs on Sunday morning, we think that will fix the lonely heart. Why?

Because we've never done anything else. We've not had to make friends before. They just came built into the structure of our church.

I say that community will not fix the lonely heart because if your spiritual connection and Peace are reliant on other people, your spiritual foundation is conditional. What happens when people inevitably disappoint you? What happens when they change or move? What happens if you tell the truth and they kick you out or reject you? If you need people to have the same spiritual practice as you, that is codependent spirituality. If you need people to approve of you, that is a codependent relationship. If you serve people because you think you must or should or because it makes you worthy, if there is any sense of guilt that motivates you, that is codependent.

I'm arguing that you don't seek out community anymore, not in the same way you did before.

I think you should seek healthy friendship. Forget community. Just focus for once on making friends.

What if you learned how to be okay on your own first? What if you processed the pain and trauma and let it go so that it wasn't the only thing you brought up on a first date? What if you figured out what felt good to you and did that? And maybe as you did that, what if you ran into people with similar interests and values to you? And what if, because you are so aligned in your purpose, so in sync with Spirit, so tapped into your Self, so turned on by your path, the people who appreciate and resonate with who you are naturally began to find you?

I will not sit here and tell you that you can think your way into attracting new people in your life. Still, the people who are supposed to come into our lives are often unable to because we don't have the emotional bandwidth to take care of anyone but ourselves. People make the mistake of thinking that if they find the right spiritual community, it will all be okay again. It's not the lack of spiritual community that is the issue.

Your lack of spiritual connection is causing the majority of your distress. Your lack of awareness is a source of more pain than you know.

I bring this up now, after three chapters on individual practice, because for you to actually enjoy any of the relationships you form from this point on, and to possibly heal any of the relationships you currently have, you need to get your individual spiritual life in order. If you want to get the full benefit of friendship or community but you aren't taking your practice into your everyday life, why are you surprised that you're struggling in the same ways as you did before? If you rely on someone else's practice or faith to get you through your life, you are re-creating the same cycle of spiritual codependence you had when you were stuck in church.

You owe it to yourself and everyone around you to get your spiritual shit together just a little bit, love.

Father Richard Rohr, a living mystic and Franciscan badass, says that the "trauma that you do not transform, you transmit." Any emotional and spiritual pain you don't compost becomes rotten, festering, more profound issues and will spill out onto your other relationships.

The answer is not to do good things in hopes that your trauma magically evaporates. The answer is to deal with your pain, and then . . . do everything else. Come into alignment with who You are, and then do what is next. Keep your practice, keep your Peace, stay in Love, and then do something as it feels right.

I'm not saying you've got to feel 100 percent good all the time to be of service or to do the right thing. But if your desire is to serve, if your desire is to give back to the world, if your desire is to see justice and equity and all the other stuff we want, it begins in and with you.

Byron Katie, a modern Wisdom teacher and living saint (if I say so myself), also says similar things in her work. If you want to end the war in the world, end the war in yourself first. If you're going to end hate in the world, stop hating yourself first. If you're going to eliminate bigotry, make sure you eliminate the bigotry you have toward yourself.

I've ruined too many relationships and friendships because of my trauma. My trauma response was activated and I yelled at people, lost their company, and felt totally justified. I lied to and cheated on a partner because I was too afraid to ask for what I wanted. I made the activist groups, the deconstruction circles, and the podcasts I listened to into my new pseudo-churches. I treated the leaders and creators like pastors when they never claimed to be those things. I held them to impossibly high standards I would never have held myself to.

Your community, friends, and people can hold space for you to heal, become, and let go. Still, ultimately and always, your individual practice and connection to Source will allow you to enjoy these relationships. Once you are able to find solace in the Love you find within your own Body, you won't demand it from others. You will not be as needy or clingy or annoyed when they won't do what you want. When you don't need people in your life to be different in order for you to be happy, you then get to enjoy the people in your life. This is freedom, beloved.

And so, if you haven't started a spiritual practice yet and you won't do it for the sake of yourself, do it for the sake of the people you claim to love. Don't you want them to have the best version of you? Don't you want to have the energy to give of yourself when the moment calls for it? Don't you want the mental space and emotional energy to help others heal? Don't you want to stand in genuine solidarity with people you claim to love?

Then do your work.

WHERE WE ARE HEADED

I noticed that when most of us deconstruct our faith or when we become more socially aware, we gain a near-instant zeal for social justice issues. Between the Trump presidency, the initial lockdown phase of the COVID-19 pandemic, and the murder of George Floyd, the number of people who flooded online spaces skyrocketed. The content creators multiplied. And suddenly, there was a whole #deconstruction community on top of an already existing #exvangelical community.

Something disheartening and strange happened a few times over in our digital spaces, on Twitter and in Facebook groups: a lot of infighting. Most of it came from a sincere desire for safety within a new communal space. I think in many of our minds, we kept thinking that we were gonna be the church, but better. We were leaving behind all the bad theology and toxic beliefs, so now we're good! We're better!

But when you put a bunch of folks with unresolved trauma in a space with limited resources to help real hurting people, shit sometimes blows up. We all know how brave people can be from behind their keyboard. We all know how an online back-and-forth can cripple your mental health for the day.

Why do we do this? Why do we keep hurting each other when we all are victims of the same system?

Because we are united by a common experience rather than a shared destination or direction.

In the case of those of us out here in the wilderness outside of traditional Christian practice, we are united by what hurt us. And we tend to fixate on what hurt us rather than dreaming of what we'd like to do different because . . . I mean, there are a zillion reasons, none of which are relevant to me. However, it all boils down to our trauma. It boils down to our need for healing on an individual level so that our collective spiritual communities can heal.

Said another way: we've got nothing to ground us. If we are to build communities, however formal or informal, they must be united by where they are going. In the last chapter, I'll offer more ideas about creating intentional community, common practice, and loose structure. But for now, let's focus on how authentic friendships lead us deeper into our spiritual path.

When I came out of the closet, I identified as a gay man and still very much a Christian. I was fortunate enough to land smack dab in the middle of some incredible queer Christian circles, never having to divorce my religious identity from my queer identity when I ultimately accepted myself. What's more, this community was also deeply dedicated to making a change in our church and in our world. In this community, I cut my teeth as a community organizer, took my first racial justice training, and realized that it would take more than good intentions to change the world. It would take intentional, organized acts of radical Love. It would take true solidarity.

My friend Alicia Crosby Mack told me how she defines solidarity in a podcast interview I did with her. "It's knowing what the water quality is." I was initially confused because that seems more like an issue for the city to deal with. But she explained that this is how close you should be if you want to be in solidarity. You should know what the water tastes like coming out of the taps in the homes of the people you seek to serve. You should know the air quality and what foods are available at the grocery store. What do they celebrate? Who is an important person to their community?

Do you know who knows details like that? Friends. Friends know that. Neighbors know these things. A family, chosen or biological, keeps track of these things. And these relationships are not one-sided like some voyeuristic missionary savior thing. They know who you are too. They know what the water quality is in your house. They know about your life and your kin because they have become your kin. People with whom you might not have a blood relation become your family. And your greatest Joy includes seeing all of them thrive, just as their happiness is in seeing you come alive.

It is from my Joy that I take action. It is from the delicious recognition that by helping secure freedom or resources for my friends, my life will also improve. So, I take these actions in a deliciously selfish way because I understand the mutual benefit. This is where the seed of friendship flowers into solidarity.

In solidarity, we share a sense of commitment to a greater vision. This answers the problem of infighting that we see in many would-be progressive spaces. Too often, we build communities based on shared experiences rather than shared vision or common goal. When that shared experience is unprocessed trauma, folks inevitably end up hurting one another to keep their sense of safety intact.

Now, while your triggers and trauma are not your fault, it is your responsibility to heal those parts of you if you want to live in Peace. Unfortunately, no one can do this for you, which is why I advocate so much for creating a spiritual practice. Because you don't have to be constantly triggered or emotionally fucked up. You don't always have to self-sabotage or mistrust people. You can change. You can become the kind of person you wish to be around, and when you do, you will naturally find the people who help foster that Goodness in you. You'll find your friends.

Your friends are the folks who share a common vision and values with you. They are the ones who are willing to help when they can. They are the ones who bring out the best in you. They are the people who are eager to listen to your suffering, who offer support when they can and hopefully call you into your wholeness. And, in an ideal world, your friends are hopefully doing their own work. Everyone is becoming more conscious, so rather than reactivating each other's trauma or constantly doing emotional labor, maybe we are laughing around a fire. Maybe we are going to a drag show or live music show. Perhaps we read science fiction or begin hiking. We start a coven and take some yoga classes.

Sometimes this will look like mutual aid, like showing up for protests, like doing what you can when you can, but more than just the political actions you take, more than the money you give during election season, more than the signs you make for the protest, do you *know* why you're doing it? Why are you showing up for these people?

Because you know two things:

You are showing up for yourself, first and foremost. And second, you love them. They are your people now. And it is because of the awareness of that Love that you keep up your inner work. This, to me, is true generosity. Not only is it easy to be generous with those you love but you have also already done the work to recognize that anything you give to a friend is not a loss. You see, there is no give and take in Love, only give and give. Only expansion.

And yes, maybe that sounds selfish. But if I am selfish for anything, it is for more of the feeling of Love's expansion. I am selfish about staying in my Peace because I want to connect with and serve the world in a way that doesn't exhaust me. I want to create more spaces for people to flourish, but never at my expense. If I want to truly serve the people around me, if I want to give them something, let me give them the most loving, kind, most connected version of me. They deserve the best from me. And so do I. I deserve to feel the most Love, the most Kindness, and the most connection.

You see how this lovely spiral of Love wraps everyone up and pulls us into a Divine dance?

Service is a path to true Joy, but performing service out of a sense of guilt will bring sorrow. And giving yourself to the point of exhaustion is not a beautiful act of service but a tragedy of your exploitation. It is not necessary. The healing of the world begins within you, and if you want to heal the world, you must first heal yourself. And as you heal, as you do the things that make you bloom, that bring you back to Peace, that make you come alive, your ability to love and serve this world will increase astronomically. You'll no longer burn out from service; your service will be sourced from your overflow.

SERVICE WITHOUT SACRIFICE

I need y'all to really understand this. We have been lied to and conditioned into believing that Love and sacrifice are bedfellows. You can't have one without the other. You cannot feel Love without first losing something. It must cost you something.

I firmly disagree. Love is generative. What you give away is secured for yourself. There is only ever an increase. This is why service is so wonderful. Those who understand genuine service give of themselves because of what it does for them. They know that the Joy they offer, the money they share, the food they cook, and the time they invest are all gifts to themselves. They feel the increase in Love and do it because they want that feeling more. It is, in a way, purely selfish.

But if the loss is felt, if discomfort is felt in service, you should question it. If a sense of exasperation is present, it would be better to not do the action because it is not actual service but a compulsion that breeds bitterness. Whether or not you realize it, people can feel the attitude you're putting off. You're nowhere near as subtle as you think.

This is why friendship is the seed we start with. Because over time you're not thinking of it as service. You're just helping your friends. And that's pretty magical, if you ask me.

As you move through your practices, you will realize that your salvation, Joy, and the greatest potential for expansion are wrapped up in the world's salvation. Said another way, your liberation and the liberation of those around you are inextricably tied together.

As we were reminded by Tricia Hersey, this is a lifelong meticulous Love practice. This is not something you need to get going all at once. It's all little bits at a time. It's choosing to care about how you feel over and over again. It's doing what will make you bloom and making no compromises. It's drawing boundaries and keeping you at the center of Love so that you can feel alive. And from that place of life, you can, once again, do anything you want.

Are you seeing how this is all pointing at the same thing? I hope so.

Part of true solidarity is bringing your authentic and most genuine Self into every space to let it be included in the process of liberation. And as you seek to be generous with what you have, joyful in who you are, you also inevitably become radically honest.

MANTRAS FOR DOPE FRIENDSHIPS

I look for people who feel like celebration.
I live within my means, and I am generous with what I have.
I bring my complete and authentic Self into every situation.
My healing is interlocked with the healing of the world.
Real solidarity looks like authentic friendship.

THINGS TO THINK ABOUT:

♦ How much of my service in the past has been driven by a sense of needing to work for my worth?

♦ What are the marks of equitable friendship?

♦ Who are the folks in my life who make me come alive? Who feels like celebration?

♦ How can I stand in more solidarity with marginalized groups? Who do I need to grow in friendship with?

THINGS TO TRY:

1. Find people who are easy to love and be around. Make it a regular point to hang out with them. This might require you to get creative, to go try a new hobby, or even phone a friend you have been meaning to talk to.

2. Cook a meal for a group of people or host a potluck dinner party. See if you can put your devices down for the entire meal.

3. Give that person money when they ask. Give more than you usually do. Don't tell anyone about it.

4. Consider the causes you give to financially and how you spend money normally. Is there a way to redirect any of that to local organizations or mutual aid?

5. Be intentional about creating space for new relationships. Go on a friendship date with someone you've been interested in spending time with.

And listen to the immersive meditation on friendship and generosity at thekevingarcia.com/bloommeditaitons.

5 | I SAID WHAT I SAID

On Radical Honesty, Defenselessness, and Kindness

> Politeness and diplomacy are responsible for more suffering and death than all the crimes of passion in history. Fuck politeness. Fuck diplomacy. Tell the Truth.
>
> —Brad Blandon, *Radical Honesty*

I don't think most people are very honest. Even the most well-meaning people. Even the sweetest, nicest people you've ever met. I don't think people in Western society know how to tell the truth very well. We lie all the time, and we just pass it off as what we do in polite society. Someone asks how you're doing. How do you respond?

"I'm good, thanks! You?"

"Oh, I'm great!" And then we move on.

Years ago, I started asking people, "How are you feeling?" Most people just answer pretty generally, but some people are shocked. What an intimate question to ask a stranger! As if I bumped up against their electric fence because no one has dared come near their heart in quite some time. Some folks get wide-eyed, and some take a second to really think, *Well, how am I feeling?* And I don't care how you answer or if you answer. I just think it's a much more interesting question.

Too many of us are walking around utterly unconscious of our feelings. Because we are unconscious of our feelings, we can never answer with any level of honesty. But as you do your work, as you keep your practices and become aware of what your physical Body feels, aware of what your energetic Body feels, you will know at any given moment where you are in relation to Peace. Are you moving closer to or further from it?

As the saying from recovery circles goes, you are only as sick as your secrets. And this goes from being a secret queer, having your faith fall apart and telling no one, to resenting people in your life for whatever reason, and yet you've never said anything in defense of your own happiness.

We learn that compliance keeps us in the group. And they call that compliance "Kindness." Worse yet, we conflate the quality of Kindness with being nice. Kindness and being nice are about being and performing, respectively. Kindness is a quality you possess and is evident when you are in the flow of who you are. Niceness is about maintaining a set of duties to preserve a fragile equilibrium. Kind is who you are. Nice is something you're trying to be.

Think of the phrase "I'm trying to be nice." This really means "I'm doing something other than what my instinct tells me to do because I think it's better and may get me what I want in the end." Maybe you learned it as a survival technique, but is it serving you now? And how many more times will you be nice instead of honest? Again, what most people are confused about is thinking that Kindness also includes compliance. They believe Kindness means never rocking the boat and never making other people uncomfortable by asking for what you need. They think

Kindness somehow means self-negation or, at worst, self-neglect for the sake of the whole flourishing.

Once again, it is not a service to the world to bring your broken Self into every situation. Your greatest gift is not the behavioral imperfections that keep you from your own Joy. Your greatest gift is your most fully healed, fully loving, most fully alive Self. And how do you become more fully alive?

By telling people what the fuck is going on inside that beautiful head of yours.

The thing that allowed me to step into my most authentic self, to own my desires and wants without shame, and to express them without regret was leaning into polyamory. And before you make me walk the plank or burn me at the stake, just take a second to breathe. I'm not saying you need to be poly or everyone needs to be poly. I am saying that *I* am polyamorous, and it has been so freeing for me to open myself up to the possibility of more Love in my life.

I grew up thinking that monogamy was the more righteous way of doing relationships. I felt it was superior. I saw what so many good Christian mothers and fathers produced, and I saw how it was the backbone of society and yadda yadda yadda. And ya know what I didn't look at? The statistic that 50 percent of all marriages, including Christian ones, end in divorce. When it finally happened in my family, I was fucking devastated; what could have possibly gone wrong?

For whatever reason, my dad wasn't happy. He wasn't satisfied for a long time, and he was dealing with so much of his own trauma that when I found him crying in the kitchen on Christmas night, I asked him what was wrong, and he told me he was leaving my mother. He packed a bag and left within the hour. That night is seared into my memory. No warning. No prep. Just a long life of keeping secrets and lying about what he really needed and wanted, culminating in a lot of pain for many people.

I wonder what would have happened if he had said sooner, "I am not happy. I think we should figure something out." Hell, what would have happened if my dad had darkened the doorway of a therapist's office? I mean, come on! Magic probably.

What would have happened if I had been honest with one of my first partners about the fact that I was worried about him moving in so soon? Or about the fact that I was still interested in having sex with other people? Or about the fact that I cheated on him shortly after we got together? What would have happened is we would have realized we wanted different things. And I wouldn't have hurt him so badly.

I thought I was being kind by hiding things from him. I thought that by maintaining a happy, steady job, trying to enjoy our time, and never bringing up the things that couldn't be fixed, I was being kind. I wasn't. I was lying. Our relationship ended in a big and spectacular blowup, as you can imagine. And I was still left with the question, "Why did I lie? Why wasn't I honest about what I wanted?"

Because I didn't want to be alone. My entire life, I had learned that to tell the truth was to be abandoned or punished. And many of us learned that. It's not our fault. But we must realize that Kindness is not equivalent to compliance. Kindness is the ability to appreciate what is without demanding the person or the situation change.

Now that we're here, on this side of our worlds falling apart, it is time to learn the fine art of direct communication and radical honesty.

THE RULES OF RADICAL HONESTY

More Than Two by Eve Rickert and Franklin Veaux, *The Ethical Slut* by Dossie Easton and Janet Hardy, and *Polysecure* by Jessica Fern are some of my favorite books on the ethical framework of nonmonogamy and polyamory. But even if you aren't a poly person, even if you are a plain old, classic monogamist, you more than anyone have something to learn from the way that poly and nonmonogamous couples structure their relationships and communicate with honesty.

Once I learned to ask for what I wanted in the bedroom and in relationships, I began taking the same principles I had in dating and relationships and applied them to the rest of my life. And I tell you, I've never been happier. I have no sick secrets, no unspoken desires, and the majority of the time, when I practice radical honesty, I usually get what I want.

One statement sums up my practice of radical honesty:

Tell the truth all the time about everything to everyone.

I try to live into three rules as a practice of radical honesty. And by rules, I mean statements or ethos. These aren't something you can break, but they are things you can fail to observe.

1. I share my feelings because I know I am responsible for taking care of my feelings.

Notice I'm not saying "immediately." Because the Lord knows, when the big emotions hit, we can feel profoundly out of control. When our feelings are peaked or triggered, we should take a step back, get grounded and centered, and then share what we are feeling. Even when, and maybe even especially when, they deserve to be verbally ripped to shreds, give it a rest.

Once I'm at a place of ease and understand my feelings, I share them. Sometimes with my therapist, sometimes with a friend, and often with the person with whom they concern. Let me make this point very clear: you don't communicate directly with someone unsafe who will make it worse. The first step is to get honest with yourself about how you feel.

In practice, I share my feelings and know that the person I'm sharing them with is not responsible for my emotions. Usually, I employ a technique I learned in Brené Brown's book *Rising Strong*: "The story I'm telling myself is . . . " The reality is, we are only ever living from the stories we tell ourselves, the dominant thought patterns in our heads. We have to be willing to question if those thoughts are even true. If we even believe them.

For example, I was having a difficult conversation with a loved one, and I started off by sharing my feelings. "The story I'm telling myself is that if I am honest with you about how I feel about our current relationship, you will start crying. Then I'm going to be resentful of you because I'm the one who needs to have a good cry. But I can't because now I think I have to take care of you. And that makes me feel so frustrated. Does that make sense?"

It doesn't even have to be that complicated. I can tell anyone how I'm feeling, and I do not need them to fix me or anything because I am keeping my personal practices of self-love and Peace and taking care of the wounded parts of me. That is no one else's responsibility. No one can fix how I'm feeling. Ultimately, I give no one the pleasure of making me feel good. That's my job, and my willingness to care about how I feel results in me getting this shit out of me, one way or another.

If someone rejects me when I share my feelings, it's okay because I can take care of me.

One time, when I wasn't sure what I felt about God or spirituality in general, I said, "Ya know, even if God doesn't love me again, I will love me forever." I want you to love you forever, to the point where you will never abandon yourself, no matter what you feel.

2. I name my needs because I know I am responsible for getting my needs met.

Dr. Christena Cleveland says in *God Is a Black Woman*, "In white-malegod's world, to be human is to be needless. So, of course, white patriarchy does not permit a definition of femininity that challenges the status quo. This is one way in which whitemalegod weaponizes femininity—by defining it as always silent and submissive to white patriarchy. In other words, if one has a need, one better keep it to oneself or only express it in ways that will not offend white patriarchy's fragile ego."

It seems simple, but not when you've been conditioned to be needless. To believe that to have a need is somehow akin to having an imperfection. The God we grew up with has a pretty intense gag reflex on anything that isn't already perfect by his standards. We keep it inside. We hide. All so we don't get punished. All so we can belong.

But that leaves me without my needs met. Allowing myself to be soft by asking for what I need doesn't make me weak or bad. It makes me deliciously human. My needs are what make me a collaborator with the rest of creation. And sure, maybe they're basic needs like rest and a good meal, but other times it's a need for connection. It's a need for intimacy, for sex. Sometimes it's a need for support, for kind words, for mutual aid. It doesn't matter. Let me ask. Because what is the worst that could happen? Someone doesn't have what I need? That's fine. I can ask someone else or figure out how to get it myself.

If the worst thing someone can say is "no" and nothing changes, that isn't too terrible, is it?

3. I can always ask for what I want if I am always okay with hearing "no."

This one is a rule directly plucked from *The Ethical Slut*. We are conditioned to never ask for what we really want because the possibility of not getting it seems horrifying. We think that unless we obtain the answer we want, we shouldn't ask it because disappointment is just too terrible to deal with.

When applied in a sexual context, being able to hear "no" from someone and not taking it personally is a huge hurdle for many folks. Myself included. It is easy to think that someone saying "no" to a sexual proposal is a "no" to me. We hear, "No, you're not good enough for me." Rejection hurts sometimes, but again, only as much as the story we tell ourselves. The reality is that nothing has changed. You asked for something, you got told no, and now. . . . what?

Well, you are responsible for your needs, wants, and desires. What would you like to do?

In all other areas of my life, this rule is magical. Not only does it allow me to be super brave, but I'm also able to assess how attached I am to an outcome based on how much the possibility of hearing "no" rattles me up.

The secret of radical honesty is letting go of the outcome of everything. Your only job in any scenario is to be honest about your feelings, needs, and wants. People may hear you, respond, and even give you what you desire, but don't count on it all the time.

This release of outcomes is also a release of fear. By releasing outcomes, we release others from the burden of having to become somebody else or do something different to make us happy. It is entering into a state of defenselessness that allows you to move through this world without tension.

ARE YOU DOING ANYTHING WRONG?

"But I feel so guilty asking for what I want and need." Why? Is it because what you are doing is wrong? Are you asking for something unreasonable? Or is it because you've been programmed your entire life to be needless?

The presence of guilt or shame always deserves interrogation and questioning. If you feel either, assess what's going on. Are you doing something that you should be ashamed of? If so. . . I don't know. Maybe fucking stop doing that? And if you can't, perhaps it's time to ask for help. But a lot of the time, the answer is probably no. You're not doing anything shameful or wrong. You've just been conditioned, and this work is about remembering what is true:

Who you are needs no defense.

A Course in Miracles says in lesson 135, "The body is in need of no defense. This cannot be too often emphasized. It will be strong and healthy if the mind does not abuse it by assigning it to roles it cannot fill, to purposes beyond its scope, and to exalted aims which it cannot accomplish." When we are not honest about who we are, we push our beautiful bodies beyond their abilities, and then we are harsh toward them when they cannot accomplish what we want.

Said another way, we are so hard on ourselves. We place enormous expectations on ourselves; we hate ourselves for not being able to do it, whatever "it" is, and then we feel bad and try again. What if we were honest about who we are and what we need, want, and feel instead? No more fighting for what we think we need or are owed. No more cowering, either. But a courageous third way, a middle way that is defenseless. Especially when we are having accusations thrown at us, when people want to manipulate us using guilt or shame, being defenseless truly becomes our strength.

To borrow from my mom: Why do you care if someone says something about you that isn't true? And it's okay that you do. You just need to realize that you're wasting energy.

Being on the internet for a while, I have had more than a few accusations thrown at me. I've been told that I ignore people's opinions, that I'm a con artist, and that I'm preying on people's insecurities to turn a buck. Many of those I just look at and shrug. I'm willing to reconsider any action I have taken if it has caused harm, but folks just not liking the content I make or how I move through the world, that isn't my problem because I am doing nothing wrong.

But what happens when you have done something wrong? What happens when someone comes to you with something serious, and you need to own your shit?

A few years back, a friend of mine texted me and asked to talk about something serious. We ended up hooking up a few years ago on New Year's Eve. I thought it was cool, consensual, and fun. We slept in separate beds and ate breakfast with a friend the following day. But in the text, he told me it took him a while to realize what happened that night.

Even though he said yes, he really wanted to say no. The sex proposal came out of nowhere for him, and in the split second that it happened, he just said yes and didn't know how to communicate that he wanted me to stop.

I felt awful. I felt dirty. I felt scared. Everything from "Oh my god, am I abusive?" to "Well, it was his responsibility to say something in the moment! How was I supposed to know?" ran through my mind. I didn't want to face the possibility that I had done something to hurt someone else. I didn't want to feel like a bad person.

It took me weeks before I could call him. I was a wreck whenever I looked at the text message I left on read. I needed to do a good chunk of work to get to a place of defenselessness before that call. If I had done something wrong, I had to be willing to hear about it and then change. And was that so bad? To have an opportunity to repair and change? And if I hadn't done anything wrong, nothing had changed. Either way, I was willing. I was willing to listen and drop my defense.

When we finished the conversation, it was clear that I didn't do anything wrong. I was merely unaware of the power dynamics between us. To him, I was a somebody with a platform and whatever, and he didn't want to disappoint me. I was under the impression that we were two adults and that yes means yes and no means no. I had clear communication and the confidence to ask for what I wanted. And he did not.

He wasn't mad at me. He just wanted to tell me so he could get free of that feeling. I apologized to him for what happened because I never tried to make him feel that way or do something he wasn't ready for. He told me he was glad he could tell me these things and I wouldn't blow up or just dodge shit.

After we hung up, I sat there, feeling lighter and more effortless. That was not nearly as stressful or draining as I thought. We both came in willing to put down our weapons and listen, to put down our defenses and look at the person in front of us. And because of this, we were able to be genuinely kind to one another and to ourselves.

THE FOUR KEYS TO KINDNESS

This kind of honesty and true Kindness may seem impossible to achieve. But it isn't. Once again, Kindness is appreciating what is without someone or something needing to change for you to be happy. It is not a thing you try and do; it is a fruit that becomes evident in your life and everyone else gets to feast on.

You might say, This is all good, but how do you do it? How the heck does this play in the real world?

The Yoga Sutras of Patanjali offers us a supreme answer:

By cultivating attitudes of friendliness toward the happy, compassion for the unhappy, delight in the virtuous, and disregard toward the wicked, the mind-stuff retains its undisturbed calmness.

You're going to run into four kinds of folks, each of them a barrier to you experiencing Peace if you respond from your defensiveness versus your defenselessness. And Patanjali offers us keys to unlock each experience so that we may maintain equanimity in our mind and Spirit. By practicing these four responses, we remain in the awareness of Love's presence and, frankly, are happier.

Friendliness toward the Happy

The number of times in my former life I looked at a happy person and scoffed because "no one could be that happy" was incredible. I was miserable as hell as I over-functioned and sacrificed my sexuality for the church. If I saw someone happy, I was convinced they were lazy or privileged or had something they were hiding. And who did that make miserable? Them or me? Instead, try to, at minimum, not be a dick. And once you get good at that, move on to an appreciation of them, their Joy. Can you share it? Can you rejoice with those who rejoice? Your jealousy does nothing to harm them and does nothing to help you. Your cynicism only keeps you locked in your pain.

The only reason it may seem challenging is that you've got a lifetime of practiced thoughts based on past experiences, which gives you every piece of data you need and every bit of justification necessary to stay where you are. My only question is, "Would you like to feel better?" This is one way.

Compassion for the Unhappy

Another translation for this is "compassion for the suffering." This one seems obvious, but if you've ever been annoyed that a person on the street asked you for money, I'd like you to check in with yourself. Have you ever had someone in your life who had so much potential and was just stuck in their own bullshit, and you'd just love to remind them they could change their life at any moment? Have you ever seen someone crying over something you think is stupid and rolled your eyes?

Our discomfort with other people's suffering is by far one of the most common blocks to Peace. We want so badly to maintain our fragile equilibrium that we will minimize the pain of others. But every bit of suffering, yours and mine, must be met with unbearable compassion. It softens us and allows us to see past the surface level.

There's also the tiny part of us that gets a little schadenfreude (the feeling or experience of pleasure at witnessing another's pain) when we see someone we've got an issue with get taken down or suffering. And I'm not saying you have to give that up, but I wonder if it's tying you to somebody you are trying to release yourself from.

Just something to think about.

Delight in the Virtuous

My guilt programming kept me in this weird pattern of secretly loathing people I admired. How was it so easy for them to keep their practice? How was it that they were experiencing so much bliss and success? And I was over here working my ass off. How is that fair? And it made me even angrier that there was nothing to hate them for! A lot of the time, they were good people, and I was jealous that it seemed so easy for them.

When you compare yourself to people who you admire, people who you perceive to be further down the road than you, further in their journey, try not to slip into the "What's wrong with me? Why can't I get this?" mindset. There's nothing wrong with you. And you don't get it yet because this shit takes time.

Developing practices and maintaining integrity takes a lifetime. And the best part is, you're never done because this is never over. Even after these bodies are done, you've got plenty of time. You've got lifetimes to cultivate what you want within you.

The people you are jealous of are showing you what you want. And that desire is the starting point of the journey ahead.

Disregard toward the Wicked

This is the hardest one for me. I'm a genderqueer human living in the South, living at the top of the twenty-first century, when the American empire is at the peak of its corruption. If you tell me to disregard the wicked, I will ask you to go bite a brick. We get nothing if we demand nothing.

Per usual, this is a yes/and situation.

Once again, this is all in the context of relationships and one-to-one interactions. Working in food service, I had to disregard wickedness all the time. The number of people in the Starbucks drive-through who treated my coworkers and me like garbage was atrocious. And I just had to continuously remind myself, "I have no idea what that person is going through to act like that." Better still, on the days I felt really holy, "Have I ever acted like that?" Not often, sure, but I know I've lost my cool on someone in public at some point. That doesn't make it right, but I understand that life is wild.

When I think of disregard toward the wicked, I think of indifference toward their hurtful actions. If I can become indifferent to them, understanding that who I am could never be threatened, I remain at Peace. And I'm better able to handle their behavior if I stay in Peace.

And that's the goal, isn't it?

When we are racially honest, we can live defenseless. When we are defenseless, Kindness becomes our nature. Kindness becomes the container for everything else we bring into our lives and all the things we keep out. When radically honest living becomes a part of our lived experience, we find that boundaries are easily created, kept, and flexible.

Our honesty is our greatest gift to the world. It is the most extraordinary Kindness. And it is so simple.

Just tell the truth to everyone about everything all the time.

MANTRAS FOR SPEAKING WITH RADICAL HONESTY

I can tell the truth to everyone, all the time, about everything.
The kindest thing I can be is honest.
I am truthful with how I am feeling, what I need, and what I desire.
Radical honesty gives me everything I want.
I can name my needs because I know I can meet my needs.
I will say what I'm feeling because I'm responsible for taking care of them.
I ask for what I want, and I'm always okay with hearing "no."

THINGS TO THINK ABOUT:

♦ Do I tend to say things exactly as they are? Or do I dance around what I want to say, hoping for someone to understand what I'm saying?

♦ Am I afraid to share my feelings with those close to me? Why is that?

♦ Do I have people in my life with whom I'm 100 percent honest?

♦ How do the rules of radical honesty feel to me? Why do they feel the way they do?

THINGS TO TRY:

1. If you talk shit constantly, you likely shit talk yourself constantly. Write down ten shitty things you have running in your head. Then right below that, write the ten opposite statements. Say these things to yourself often, daily even, as part of your practice.

2. Think of someone you admire, the qualities you find attractive in them. How are these qualities already present in you?

3. What are three things you have been afraid to say out loud to yourself or someone else? Write those things down. Why are you afraid to say these things? Write that down too.

4. Make it a point to share at least one of those three things with a trusted person in your life.

5. Look at yourself in the mirror naked and tell yourself that you love yourself.

And listen to the meditation on radical honesty and Kindness at thekevingarcia.com/bloommeditations.

NO MATTER WHAT

6

On Boundaries, Unbearable Compassion, and Patience

You don't protect your heart from breaking because in a way a broken heart is like cracking a shell to let the deeper heart come forth.

—Ram Dass, "Unbearable Compassion" (blog post),
Be Here Now Network

Growing up, my family had a rule: we don't lock doors inside the house. On the one hand, I think it was because my family was afraid that if one of us was hurt and locked inside the room, they didn't want any barriers in the way of them getting to us. But the implicit message I got was that I didn't have a right to privacy. There was nothing that was mine, not completely. The church echoed this sentiment by often compelling us to share our dark secrets with people who didn't have our best interest or the capacity to hold such giant sums of energy with care and grace.

So many of us, myself included, tend to waffle on our boundaries, what we are willing to and not willing to engage with because we're so starved for Love that even a bitter thing tastes sweet to us.

Boundaries are the seeds that allow for unbearable compassion to blossom within us. We create the space, the atmosphere, and the conditions for this flower to bear the fruit of Patience. When we set healthy boundaries, we create more opportunities to let go of our pain because we're not in a constant state of hypervigilance due to feeling triggered or on guard for the next threat. We grow in understanding about why we behaved the way we did, and because we understand ourselves, we can understand why everyone else is acting the way they do. Our unbearable compassion for ourselves gives us Patience for the world around us and those in it. We become more content, knowing that no one has to change us to experience Peace, and we understand that the more Love we give, the more Love we reap.

We can love people by telling them exactly what we need, want, and desire, including the need (and it is a need) to be loved and treated with Kindness. Now that we've gotten a taste of that, our capacity for loving ourselves has expanded, and we understand the power our unbearable compassion has in our healing. There's no going back. Once your feet have felt the promised land, you couldn't dream of going back. But what do we do when we are around people who trigger us? Who don't understand us and want us to be different than who we are? We revert to old ways of being. Our hearts break each time we let our family members, old church friends, or anyone talk poorly about us and our journey.

And I understand why I did that and sometimes still do that: I want to be loved. But I'm under the delusion that I wish for that person's Love. It's nice, but it can't satisfy. Only living water, only the Love that we find in our stillness, will heal us. We must remind ourselves, over and over, as many times as we need, to have unbearable compassion for the soft animal of our Body for wanting what they want, loving what they love, even if it hurts.

That unbearable compassion births a cosmic Patience that just keeps expanding. Your mistakes are no longer "OMG, what a fuck up," but "OMG, of course, I would do that. I've been stuck on that for a while. I'm so glad I can care for myself through this."

When you understand the depths of your own need for compassion, you naturally extend compassion to others. You care less about other people's poor behaviors, not because you don't want them to do the right thing, but because you understand how being disconnected from Love feels. Your understanding will bring you Peace; ultimately, you can choose to engage with the pain of this world from a place that will never be unsettled.

DIE-HARD

Old habits are a real bitch. And I mean that for both the things we do and the things we think. Our old habits are never more clearly on display than in our relationships, who we interact with, how we treat them, and how we allow them to treat us. When we begin spiritual recovery, it is not uncommon for us to become a little (or a lot) more intolerant of being treated like shit by people around us. And when I tell you how people get so bent out of shape by the mild inconvenience of you not doing as they ask! At first, I was mortified any time I remotely disappointed someone. Now I find it exhilarating.

As I said before, my over-functioning habits continued into my late twenties. I was also hustling my ass off to pay bills because I worked as a server and a social media manager for a few nonprofits, and I'd take on anything that people would pay me for if it was even remotely within my ability. I was working too many hours for too little pay. And little by little, I began falling apart. Projects fell through. I'd forget things that needed to be done. Dates would just blank out in my mind. And I felt a lot of shame. One day I sat down with my friend Crystal, someone I was working for at the time, and she said, "Kevin, I think you're overworking, and it's causing my work to suffer. And I want you to step back right now, reevaluate what you can do, and if it feels right, come back." No shame. No blame. Just a clear recognition that the way I was operating was unsustainable.

Too many of us are shamed for our lack of productivity. And too many of us are not considering that we all are (still) living through a global pandemic. It's kept many of us isolated for three years or longer. There's an economic collapse happening all over, and the United States government is constantly dancing on a knife edge between late-stage capitalism collapse and total Christofacism. We are stressed. And our collective capacity ain't what it used to be.

We've covered the reasons to keep yourself in the center of your Peace, and now I'm asking you to find your nonnegotiables. What are the things you're doing that are working for you? What practices are grounding you, making you feel good, and making you come alive? And if it's still nothing, I invite you to try the practices I have offered in this book as a road map until you get your bearings in your own spiritual path.

If you want to feel Peace, if you want to get over your triggers and stop being obsessed with your past, your spiritual practice must become your nonnegotiable. It must be a boundary in your life. It must be the container in which everything is poured, mixed, alchemized, and transformed.

This need not be complicated. And I believe we could sum up our lives with one simple boundary, one simple intention: I want to remain in Love and at Peace. Therefore, anything that takes me out of that awareness of Love, anything that pulls me out of my Peace, I need to question whether or not to give it my attention. Sounds simple enough, right? But the practice of this is what gives people trouble. A half-hearted commitment to your Peace, to the Peace of your Body, leads to suffering.

But there is a way out.

By practicing radical honesty, I'm clear about who I am and what I want. I can communicate those things clearly to people in my life, and I know I am responsible for taking care of that need and following those desires, should they lead to beneficial things. The communication that comes from radical honesty helps establish clarity, and where there is clarity, a natural boundary often forms. I don't usually need to be clearer than being clear.

What's more, these natural boundaries are not created as a defense. There is nothing that needs defending here. True Peace is such that in its presence, there is nothing that is not dissolved and brought into it. I see Peace as a garden with large trees that border it. There are rows of cultivated flowers, wild vines, and beautiful flowing water. This is where I stay, in my Peace, surrounded by beauty. Outside the boundaries of my garden, I hear the scary sounds of those clamoring for me to come see.

Look what they did to me.
Look what they are doing to us.
They are going to come for you too.
Aren't you afraid that this could be taken from you?

No. I am not. Because here in this space, in the garden of my heart, I am at Peace and at ease. If I go out to see the world's troubles, if I leave my Peace to help someone else in distress, what am I offering? If I look upon the stress of your life and commiserate with you about all the shit happening, and believe me, I know it is happening, am I helping either of us move toward more Peace or Joy?

I am open to hearing of your sorrow, do not mistake me. There is room for all of it. And after that, after you've made the space for the pain to stretch out within you and release, what shall we do? If I were sitting with you, I'd invite you into a space of Peace and deep compassion to examine the things that cause you pain. Sit in your own garden with your sorrow, angst, and anger. Sit and let all those things compost into nutrients for the soil of your heart.

Now, how does this look practically?

For me, I want to feel Peace. That is my bottom line 100 percent of the time. So I don't engage with shit that disturbs it. When I am disturbed, that is a sign that I have forgotten who and what I am. It is an invitation to return to my practice.

Imagine you work at a restaurant. It is nearing the holiday season. You've requested time off in the summertime because you know how hard it is to get that approved last minute. You make all your plans. You book your flights. And the week before, the new schedule drops, and you're scheduled every day you are gone. You go to your boss to inquire, and they say they can't approve the time off because *they* are going out of town for their vacation, and an extra person is needed to run the shift.

"You're new here. And everyone has to work this kinda shift every now and again." What do you do?

Well, I'll tell you what I want to do. This was an actual situation I went through. And as an enneagram 8 and a Scorpio, I want to protest! This is bullshit! I requested this off in June, and you're *just now* telling me, after I spent all this nonrefundable money to go home? I'm not paid enough at this job to stick around. I might as well just quit and find a new job when I get back. Fuck this.

That's my knee-jerk response. This is what I think would initially feel really good. Dramatic. Power play. And maybe I'll get what I want if I pitch a fit. Super mature, right?

Now, what I actually did: I calmly explained that I had already purchased the ticket to go home and told my family I'd be there. I offered to look for people to cover the scheduled shifts, but the ones I couldn't get scheduled would have to go short one person "because I will not be here, regardless of the schedule. I'm so sorry. I do wish I could be more help." My boss was not pleased. But I kept my job. I did find people to cover the shifts. I did go home. And I didn't lose my Peace in the process.

I got what I wanted, which was to remain in Peace. Easy, right? Simple enough. But what if the person you are dealing with is super antagonistic? What if the person is your family member and they are being hateful toward you? What if they've been doing it for years? And what if you've been quiet about it up to this point?

Well, just ask yourself again what you want. Do you want to feel Peace? Are you willing to do what is needed to attain and keep it? If the answer is yes, then all you need to do is ground yourself.

THE PRICE OF ADMISSION

Think back to the last time you went to a carnival or a fair. You probably paid a price of admission. The ticket to get in cost something. So did the hay ride and the corn maze. The games cost tickets, which also cost money, as did the big Ferris wheel. And you knew what you were getting for your money. You knew that you were paying at least $60 at this thing for a killer fight with heartburn, but also, maybe, some fun.

Similarly, every relationship in your life has a price of admission. Going in, playing the games, or being with said person costs you something. In healthy relationships, there are equitable exchanges of energy. We give our attention to someone, we hold them as the object of our positive attention, and hopefully they do the same for us. These exchanges should give us Joy, connection, fulfillment, and validation. But many times, relationships based on compulsion rather than free choice result in more stress. We end up working on relationships instead of being in them. We lose more than we gain. And we stick around in these relationships longer than we should because we think that sacrifice and Love go hand in hand. We believe that sacrifice *is* Love.

But in perfect Love, there is no give and take. There is only give and give. There is only a generative exchange. Relationships at their best feel like this. But more than likely, your relationship isn't perfect. (Imagine that!) So for those of us who fluctuate, have mood swings, and get cranky when we don't eat, it is a give and take. Sometimes we're in abundance and have the emotional energy to give. Sometimes we're in a spiritual or emotional lack and we need someone to pour into us. Thus, every relationship has a price of admission. The only question is, "Am I willing to pay the price?"

Think about your best friends. What's the price of admission to be with them? Likely it's not too high. Maybe you tell the truth, be yourself? Maybe spend time with them and be encouraging? Perhaps you enjoy things together? It costs you some energy, time, and attention, but there's also so much value in this exchange, isn't there? That's a good deal.

And they have to ask the same of you. What's the cost of being friends with you? Do you require a certain kind of attention? Or time? Do you need them to be voting in the same direction as you? Do you need them to enjoy the same things as you? Sure! Maybe. These are all very shallow ideas, but friendship can be that simple if we like it to be. The deeper the relationship, though, usually built over time and through shared experiences, the greater the expectations we sometimes have.

Have you ever gotten too intense with a friend? You lean really hard on them for a season, and then that season just keeps going, and then they start getting tired of always hearing about your suffering? And you might think, "OMG, my friend isn't making space for me to feel my feelings? My friend doesn't care! My friend has changed! They are so fucked up."

Yes. Your friend did change. And so did you. You both are changing all the time. And you are expecting them to behave in a way that meets your needs and wants, and they may not want to do that. And that is their prerogative. So, you're asking them for something they do not have. You say, "To be with me, you must witness this endless sorrow without protest." And that might be too high a price for your friend. Maybe they don't have the emotional depth to handle what you went through and hold you through it.

And that is okay. It has to be. Because if we remember our rules of honesty, we remember that though we can always name our feelings, we know we are responsible for taking care of them. I can ask my friend for what I need, and they can say no, and I'm okay with that because I know where the responsibility for my life lands.

Let them off the hook for your happiness. You will also be happier.

Now that I've torn you a new one, let us turn to some folks closer to home. Your family, your partner, your church, or your spiritual community. There is an admission price. What is it?

Do you have to hide any part of who you are? Do you have to edit what you say in real time, stop yourself from gasping at someone's racism, sexism, or homophobia? Do you have to perform your happiness when you're miserable? Do you have to hide your joyful feelings or your natural flamboyance? Do you have to lie about anything for any reason?

And how long have you been paying for that? How does it make you feel to pay such a price?

As you continue to grow in your spiritual practice, as you begin to grow in the awareness of Love's presence, you may find yourself less and less willing to pay the price for specific relationships. And that's a good thing.

When we encounter an impasse or conflict with those we love, we must do what scares us the most. And it is this:

We have to fucking communicate what's going on inside with radical, explicit honesty. No matter what. And we do this because anything else will keep us stuck in our suffering. Most of our friends, family, and loves aren't psychics or mind readers. Otherwise, they would have done something by now.

This is how I move through difficult and downright shitty hard conversations:

1. I breathe and ground myself. I usually make sure I've meditated that day and set my intention: I wish to seek Peace for myself and this person I love. Nothing more.

2. When I come to the person, I ask for two things. First, "Can I share how I am feeling first, and you just listen? And then you respond?" And second, "I don't want us to yell at each other because we love each other. And if we can't keep that rule, me especially, I think we should revisit this another time."

3. I share how I've been feeling. How long it's been going on. The work I've tried to do on my own to let it go, but "the story I'm telling myself is . . ." (to borrow from Brené Brown's *Daring Greatly*), and then I usually end with, "And I don't know if any of that is true, but it's been making me feel awful." Because it is. And then I invite them to tell me what's been going on from their perspective.

So often, our issues stem from an inability to communicate rather than people being jerks to each other. So often, we can ask for what we want, the thing we think is so much, so costly, and people may be willing to give it to us.

But what about when they can't? What if we ask for something and they don't want to give it to us, even though they have it to give?

My real-life example is from my coming out as queer to my family. Had they not been open and affirming and totally loving, I would have communicated to them how I wanted to be treated for me to be able to be around them. It might sound something like,

> "I understand that we disagree on this. I don't need you
> to be affirming of me or my sexuality or my relationships
> for me to be happy. I just need you to treat me, my friends,
> and my partner with Kindness and compassion. And if that
> can't happen, our relationship will have to change."

That's the big thing in all this: I'm doing this for myself. I really do not need anyone to change for me to be happy. But if I am going to stay happy, I need them to treat me with compassion and Kindness at a minimum. That is *not* a huge ask. However, people love to define what compassion and Kindness are for them. So you might need to be more specific.

> "When I'm around, you can't talk disparagingly about
> queer people or things you don't like about LGBTQ folks
> unless you want me to leave."

> "When my partner is here with me on holidays,
> we will sleep in the same bed or we can find other
> accommodations."

> "You will not keep evangelizing me every time we hop on
> the phone, otherwise I am gonna pick up less and less."

"I will not tolerate you disrespecting Black people by making racist jokes."

"I don't feel good about staying around you when you refer to women as bitches and refer to men who don't act like you as 'betas.' Also that's real fucking stupid."

"You will use his/her/their correct pronouns when referring to my friend/sibling, or we simply won't be speaking as much."

Whatever it is, whatever your ask is, you have to be clear. Not demanding but clearly stating that if you can't get what you need here with this person (and likely it's just Kindness and us not treating each other like assholes), your relationship will change. I've never had to specify what that means because I've never had to. I've merely acted.

I've asked for respect.
I have been refused respect.
And that person didn't see me again.

I started giving more attention to people and things that make me feel good. And I offered less and less attention to people and things that were draining my energy. Even if I had been connected to those people or things for years. I couldn't keep living in ways that made me shrink, which caused me to feel stressed and worried. And not because I didn't love those people but because I can't love them very well when I'm angry with them.

If I cannot be in someone's presence and treat them with Kindness, I have no business being near them. And if someone disrespects me, I will more likely not be kind to them. So, of course I don't wanna be near them. But again, they don't need to change. They often don't know how. They usually can't. But I will love myself no matter what. I will care for this Body no matter what.

UNBEARABLE COMPASSION

I've heard Ram Dass tell this story in a few of his talks about a statue of Buddha bearing a smirk. It's called the "Buddha with the Smile of Unbearable Compassion." And people who see it are said to burst into tears, feeling the loving understanding of the Buddha, who sees all of our drama and suffering but does not drop down into it with us. He smiles, inviting us back into Peace. With unbearable compassion, we are drawn back to Love. The sweet Kindness draws our hearts to repentance, to change our minds.

That idea of unbearable compassion has stuck with me and has grown into a principle I hold dear. I think of how a parent looks at a child upset with something seemingly banal. But the mother doesn't try to explain to the toddler the minutia of this moment, that all suffering will not last forever, or that this child should just let go of their attachment to the situation and be free. No, the mother picks up the child while they are wailing and says, "Oh, sweet baby, come here. I know it hurts, but I am here. It will be okay. Everything will be okay."

And eventually, the child stops crying, comforted by their mother's embrace, or because they've worn themselves out. Regardless, the result is resting in Love's arms. We are not so different.

We are still just as tender as we were as babies. We have moments when we put on the mask of a grown-ass adult. We act like we are over things. We practice resilience to survive, but my love, the part of you that has been denied sweetness needs your unbearable compassion. As we were trained to be good boys and girls, good citizens, good capitalists, good adults, we learned that maturity meant never letting your emotions slow down your productivity. We learned that pain is weakness leaving the Body. We learned that we should just get over it. But we're not over it, and we beat ourselves up because we shouldn't be bothered by things that are bothering us.

We think we need to be holier than we are, rather than recognizing that our Goodness, our Holiness, our light are never dimmed by a shit attitude or a moment of fear.

Having unbearable compassion for myself means I will love myself through every feeling. I never condemn. I meet it all with loving understanding because I understand entirely why I feel the way I do. I know exactly why I'm hurting, and I will still love me, even if I don't know why. I'm gonna do the work of holding myself in Love.

And that, my friends, is called Patience. By the time I've placed the boundaries and been clear about what I need, by the time I've got the unbearable compassion moving, Patience for myself becomes effortless.

I'm patient with myself because I know that things are hard. I know I can't be expected to stay in the flow all the time, so why would I ever be unkind to myself? Why would I define my perfection by a lack of contrast or conflict? Why would I? Unless I believe something untrue.

And that's where it clicks for me: if I believe something wild, if I have a practiced thought pattern or decades-old habit, then it makes sense that I would behave in a certain way. It makes sense that I would still struggle with what I struggle with, given that I've only recently begun trying to change my behavior by addressing the pain underneath it all. I've gotta cut myself some slack.

Now, here's where we take it even further.

Can you recognize that everyone is doing the same thing? That all the people you have issues with, all the would-be idiots of the world, are only acting out of the stories they believe? You say, "They shouldn't act that way." I say that it makes perfect sense they are acting this way. Given their life, their story, and what they have been doing up until this point, if they'd act any different, I'd be surprised. With that in mind, I can either resent them or meet them with some of the compassion I'm giving myself. I must see them where they are, and to love them unconditionally, with unbearable compassion, to have Patience with them, I must also have boundaries.

None of this justifies poor behavior, but it does explain it. And will I spend my time trying to educate someone who doesn't want to learn? Do I want to give my energy, make the space within me, to include this person's growth edges? Sometimes the answer is yes. But often, as we go through our healing journey, we are willing to tolerate less and less. And that's a good thing.

You are learning to own your space. Your Body. Your choices. You are taking responsibility for your own happiness. You realize that no one can make the life you want but you. And sweetie, you're allowed to let go of the things and people that can't come along with you. Trust me, you are so worth it.

MANTRAS FOR CREATING HEALTHY BOUNDARIES

I love myself so much and am dedicated to keeping myself in Peace.
My boundaries are made of Love.
Saying no to what I can't abide is saying yes to the things that make
me come alive.
I can tell when relationships aren't reciprocal, and I adjust accordingly.
I feel the unbearable compassion of God for me.

THINGS TO THINK ABOUT:

♦ What's my relationship with boundaries? Do I keep them, or do I make them and break them?

♦ What is the price of admission with my family? With my significant other(s)? With my friendship group? My spiritual community?

♦ Do I notice any imbalance in my relationships?

♦ What do I need to say no to? What do I want to say yes to?

THINGS TO TRY:

1. Before going into a hard conversation, rehearse the opening requests of "May I speak first?" and "We're not going to yell at each other." Make sure those are clear. Also, write down some points you may want to cover in any difficult conversation, especially if you get nervous or emotional and lose track of your objective.

2. Write down a few things you beat yourself up over, the things that really hit you in your shame triggers. What is it about those things that triggers you so much? Can

you notice your big reaction next time and instead give yourself unbearable compassion?

3. Write two letters. One from your younger self, who still feels unsafe and is in need of some big Love. And one from you now, telling your younger Self about how you're going to help both of you heal. Read these letters out loud to yourself.

4. Unfollow and block folks on the internet who continually violate your boundaries. Do this liberally and with all gusto. And then if you're feeling real petty, make another post about how you just blocked a bunch of folks to protect your Peace.

5. Finish this sentence: I want to be more patient with . . .

And listen to the immersive meditation on compassion and Patience at thekevingarcia.com/bloommeditations.

7 | LET THAT SHIT GO
On Surrender, Forgiveness, and Peace

It is because you have made [your sibling] a stranger that you are afraid of [them]. Perceive [them] correctly so that you can know them. There are no strangers in God's creation.

—A Course In Miracles,
T-3.III.7:5–7

Peace. I've been talking about it this entire time, and here it stands as its own thing. By now, I hope you understand what I mean when I say Peace. I hope you've felt it. And if there's any place in your life where there isn't Peace, I want you to go there and begin freeing yourself from whatever is holding you back.

Growing up, if things were peaceful, not hectic, and I wasn't busy doing something for white Jesus or the church, I would start to worry. Idle hands were said to be the devil's playground, so I only allowed myself to feel okay when I was moving. Once again, I was bamboozled into thinking that Peace was some far-off thing I had to work for and that I wasn't worthy of without suffering first.

Peace is not a thing you do. Peace is your natural state when you are aligned with who you are created to be. It should be evident to you if you are experiencing it. But if it's not, then friend, you've spent a lot of time in an activated state of stress. What would it be like to let that go? To let go of everything, every thought that is hurting you? What would it be like to surrender to what is instead of struggling against it so hard? What if you let yourself embrace the unknown a bit instead of fighting against something that isn't fighting back?

I've mentioned a few times that I'm a Scorpio and an enneagram 8. If you know anything about the zodiac or enneagram, you know that giving up the fight is not something folks like me do with any grace. It's not in our blood to give up. To admit defeat. And it's certainly not in us to naturally admit when we are wrong. We've never seen a fight not worth fighting. And while it can make a bitch like me feel hella powerful, it is certainly not peaceful.

Sitting in my therapist's office once, I was recounting once again, for the umpteenth time, how that one pastor at my last church hurt me, lied to me, and betrayed me. I was so mad that he didn't see the damage he had caused. I was furious that I was discriminated against for being who I was. I was livid that this guy was a fair-weather friend, only showing up for me when it was good for him. And I hated that I knew this was who he was before I even began trying to grow in friendship with him, hoping that he would change his mind and our church. I knew he didn't hold an affirming theology or praxis. I knew that he was a church pastor in a conservative congregation, and his job rested on his ability to never change or grow, to never challenge the status quo. And yet I entered into this relationship anyway.

Why? Knowing I'd likely be betrayed, I still insisted on investing my time in him and this church. Why did I do this? Not a clue. Perhaps an unconscious pattern making me believe that undue suffering should be rewarded? As if he should change to make me happy because that's how I'd operated my entire life? There are a million reasons possibly, but none of them matter in the face of the question my therapist asked me next.

"Well, do you wanna be right? Or do you want to be happy?"

"Why can't I have both?"

"Because he'll never think you're right or that he did wrong. And you've lamented this for a few sessions now, and I'm just wondering if you think letting it go might make you happier? 'Cause you can't hold on to that anger and be happy."

I stared wide-eyed at the ground. My therapist was right. My mind immediately jumped to, "But he hurt me. He's wrong in this. I was sinned against. I'm the victim here. Don't put this on me." But she wasn't doing that. She was just asking if I would like to be happy rather than right.

Given the two, I suppose I'd like to be happy.

This dude took up so much of my brain space. It was like that scene in the movie *Mean Girls*, when Cady is monologuing to herself about how she became obsessed with Regina George, even though she claimed to hate her. "I couldn't stop talking about her. And when I wasn't talking about her, I was thinking of a reason to bring her up in conversation . . . and I could hear people getting bored with me."

That was me. Forever talking about this asshole pastor who hurt me. And forever feeling miserable because I wanted something I couldn't have.

And I could hear people getting bored with me. Including me.

HANDS UP

A prayer I borrow from *A Return to Love* by Marianne Williamson simply reads, "I forgive you . . . and I release you to the Holy Spirit." That's how your surrendering begins. That's how letting it go starts. A minimal acknowledgment, but a powerful one. This person has been living in your head, rent-free, for how long? And now you are intentionally trying to fill your mind with other things, intentionally trying to turn your attention to something else. In some ways, you're trying to forget about them, or at least the actions or the pain you associate with that memory.

Do you know why it hurts to keep thinking and talking about it? Because this isn't something that needs to be spoken or thought about any longer. It's not a mental issue to solve but an emotional one. There's nothing to do, everything to feel.

Start off by acknowledging whatever you feel. You feel angry, petty, and upset. You feel sad, depressed, and disturbed. Whatever the feeling is, let it be here. Feel it as much as you need to. And then, when you've really let it ruminate and you understand it, let the simple question float to your mind.

"What can I do to feel better right now? Do I want to feel better?"

The answer might be no. One time, I was in a bad spot, so I called my friend RV, who is not one to put up with my bullshit for too long, and he dragged me with a question. I was going on and on about trying to feel better, but I just couldn't shake this feeling off me. "Kevin, do you wanna throw a pity party? Do you wanna just be fucking sad for a bit?"

Yeah! Yeah, I do wanna be fucking sad for a bit.

"Okay, go do that." We hung up. I proceeded to cry and watch cartoons. After about an hour of this, I felt better and decided to drink water and eat. Things quickly improved. I thought about what was causing me to be here, the story in my head causing me to feel miserable. And then I took a deep breath and said, "I love you, and I release you to the Holy Spirit."

Sometimes I just can't do it. I can't heal this right now. I can't handle this. I have to give this to God, to the Universe to handle. And later on, I say the same prayer when I realize I'm still carrying whatever it is. And when I go further and realize I picked up whatever it is again, I lay it back down. It's coming back, again and again, because I want to be happy. I don't want to carry these heavy things anymore. I want to let the pain of my past go.

That, my friends, is called forgiveness.

THE ONLY PERSON YOU NEED TO FORGIVE

Too many of us have a fucked-up view of forgiveness. We were told we must forgive our enemies. We were convinced that we must pray for those who hurt us. We were taught that reconciliation was the highest form of forgiveness, and that anything less than a complete restoration of the relationship was imperfect and, therefore, unacceptable. The verses in the Bible are so easily used to manipulate and gaslight people that we tend to push the concept of forgiveness away. Because the people who hurt us do not deserve our forgiveness.

And I'd agree. They do not deserve it. And I won't even tell you to forgive them for your sake. But you do need to learn how to let them go.

ACIM talks deeply about forgiveness from the perspective of your well-being and no one else's. "Forgiveness is the healing of the perception of separation." If I am distressed, angry, sorrowful, if I feel anything but the Peace of God, if I am not feeling Love, do I want to return to it? Do I want to shift my perception from fear to Love so I can finally feel better?

If I want to heal my perception of separation, I need to forgive myself for believing myself separate.

I'm in pain when I think of that asshole pastor who hurt me. He's not. I'm putting myself back in that painful mindset, allowing my memories to become real and reliving them time and time again. The reality is, that pastor only broke my heart one time. But in my head, he did it thousands of times. Hundreds of times in a day, even. Every time I revisit that and let the scenario play out the same script, it becomes a chronic thought pattern I can't seem to break away from.

He's never going to change. So what can I do? When there is no justice to be found? When there is no way to get what I want?

I need to let that shit go. I need to forgive myself for allowing this person to take up so much space in my life, for believing that this dude with barely any credentials and zero empathy could make me feel so miserable all these years later. I remind myself that the past is over and it can't touch me anymore. The thoughts in my head are not reality now. They are only showing me how I suffered. But I can forgive my mind. It's only trying to protect me too.

My shift in thought patterns didn't happen all at once. It took years before I stopped talking about that shitty church that hurt me. As stated before, this is a lifelong meticulous Love practice, so don't push yourself to magically be over it. We're not in a hurry here. You're not gonna get over it. You'll just let it flow through you. You'll surrender it little by little every time you shift your attention from what caused you pain to what makes you bloom.

Those of us with deep-seated pain, the stuff that's been with us a long time, should not be surprised by the fact that the same shit comes up multiple times during our healing journey. You should expect it to come up as often as it needs to. And it's not like you're not healing. There's just more. There's deeper healing. And it will come back around as often as needed until you learn the lesson. Do not be angry or upset about this. I laugh whenever I've got one of my old triggers or old shitty things that come up again. I say, "Of course I would do that. Of course I would feel that way."

Slowly, though, as you keep your practice, find your people, and fall more deeply in Love, you'll surrender your ghosts. You'll forgive yourself for whatever you think you did or didn't do, and then you'll finally be doing something else instead of constantly rehashing your pain.

You'll find that the more compassion you have for your suffering, the easier it is to forgive, and the easier it is to forgive, the quicker you'll find yourself in Peace.

THE DEEPER WORK OF UNDERSTANDING

It all starts with you. You must do the work of forgiving yourself if you hope to forgive someone else. You must return to your Self to find a path through forgiveness. Again, I don't think it's what we've been told.

Forgiveness is a recognition of reality without wishing it were different. This requires us, annoyingly, to be the bigger human.

We have to go to the ten-thousand-foot view of the situation to see us and the person or situation we are having an issue with in its fullness. When I step back and view myself from ten thousand feet, I can see how I escaped some shitty relationships, that those folks were not treating me right. I can see how they manipulated me and how I fell for the promise of belonging. I can see how my genuine desire to serve God was co-opted by folks who had no idea what they were doing.

I see my former leaders and pastors. I know the life they've lived. I see how their privileged identities keep them stuck in a limited understanding of God's work on the earth and how they are inexorably tied to the success of their local social club they call a church. I can see how they were so scared to do the right thing, and rather than leaning into Love, they fell back into fear and did what would keep the church doors open.

I see it. I understand why they did what they did. I don't like it. But I know that given where they are, they couldn't have done anything differently. The ego will protest, "YES, THEY COULD HAVE!" But . . . wouldn't they have done something different if they could? And that feels so gross to admit that these people who hurt me, my enemies . . . are human. And they are more afraid of God than I've ever been. They are stuck in their fear, and I move from anger to pity when I see that.

> Pity that they refuse to love bigger, even though they know they could.
> Pity that they are stuck in a system that disallows them from growing or changing.

Pity that they lost me as a friend because a reputation with other rich white people was more important than their queer friend who just wanted to be treated equally in their church.

Pity. Because they will miss out on the glory that I am.

I DON'T KNOW HER

One of the most incredible interview clips of all time is when Whitney Houston is asked what she thinks of the new starlet on the scene, Mariah Carey.

"What do I think of her?" Whitney repeats. "I don't."

I don't think of her.

Damn. Freaking icon.

That's what I feel about most folks in my past. Occasionally, a person will ask me, "Did you hear about what he did?" They'll update me on the latest gossip or drama in my old church. And I'll shrug and say, wow, that's neat, okay, cool, because frankly, I'm not thinking about them anymore. They take up less than 1 percent of my headspace now because I'm busy trying to figure out what I wanna do. I'm busy focusing on what makes me happy, what makes me bloom, and what brings me Peace beyond understanding.

Peace, my friends, that's what's waiting for us on the other side of our captured thoughts. And it happens in the most deliciously subtle way.

In the winter of 2020, when the coronavirus pandemic was still in its earliest stages, my pod of five friends was gathering to watch our version of competitive sports: Ru Paul's Drag Race. I ran to the grocery with my mask to grab some fried chicken and potatoes because I'm from the South and that's what we do. I took off my mask when I exited the store and loaded my items into the back seat when I heard, "Kevin?"

A quick spin revealed the voice belonged to that asshole pastor I've been talking about this entire chapter. I hadn't seen him in ages.

The last time I ran into him was at my favorite coffee shop. He would be there from time to time with his posse, doing Bible studies or doing "sermon" prep (I've got opinions about his preaching) or something stupid, I'm sure. What drove me mad was that he acted like nothing mattered, like he had done nothing wrong in our relationship. It was as if he didn't realize that he had devastated my entire life when everything blew up. I'm reasonably sure he didn't. Either that or his white boy pretty privilege made him think he could talk to me.

That last time we saw each other, he asked me how I was.

"My dad died," I responded and stared blankly at his face.

He didn't know how to react. And I got my coffee and left without a goodbye. I was so annoyed by him. He was so clueless and heartless. What a poor excuse for a pastor, I thought to myself.

Back to the parking lot: He called my name, I turned around, looked at him, and it took me a few moments to register who he was in my head, as if he was someone who I had met at a thing once. Once I recognized him, I wasted no time excusing myself.

"So, how have you been?" He asked from his car's rolled-down window.

"Never been happier in my life," I responded. " . . . I'm going to go now."

As I circled my car to get in the driver's seat, he called, "Good to see you!"

To which I responded, "Uh huh!"

And I drove away. I turned up the music, and as the car accelerated, I started laughing hysterically about what had just happened. That asshole thought he could have my time, and I didn't give him any. I hadn't thought about him in years. Someone who I was obsessed with, who I wanted so badly to change, who hurt me and so many of my friends, this guy was now a blip of recognition. Did I excuse him? Did I make him feel better about what he did? Absolutely not. But did I let him ruin the rest of my night?

Also no.

I had done the work to find people who loved me, and I stopped fixating on the people who hurt me. I had created new spiritual practices in my life that were not triggering, so I stopped focusing on the churches that betrayed me.

It wasn't a matter of needing to get over, forget, or even forgive someone.

It was simply shifting my focus.

I was laughing hard because I didn't even realize how free I'd become. I was gonna go home and watch Drag Race with a bunch of my queer friends. We were gonna smoke some weed and crack open some beer while we cracked jokes about each other. And this guy didn't get to be a part of that.

I had forgiven myself for thinking he was responsible for making me happy. He could keep doing his asshole thing, and I would be satisfied.

THE NEXT BEST THOUGHT

Is that forgiveness? No longer letting the past haunt your mind by coming here to the present? Just forgetting about the people and things that hurt you? I think maybe. It becomes a lot more straightforward. You ain't gotta let nothing go. You ain't gotta actively absolve someone of their sins. You just shift focus.

And when you find yourself fixated again, you shift focus again. Moment by moment. Situation by situation. Slowly. Just forgetting about the shit that doesn't truly matter to you anymore. Remembering what fills you with Peace.

This is not a carte blanche to spiritually bypass your suffering, BTW. This is a means of processing it. If it keeps coming up, you're still clinging to it. And that's fine. Just keep letting go. Keep giving yourself compassion.

"But what if I can't let it go?" Then don't. Don't let anything go that you don't wanna let go. Keep holding on to it, rehashing it, and doing it as long as it makes you happy. And if you're stuck here, don't try to get unstuck. It's like a finger trap toy. The more you resist what's happening, the more you pull away from it, the more stuck you are. But the more you relax, the more you lean in, the easier the release becomes.

Abraham Hicks, a modern Wisdom teacher and author of several spiritual self-help books, including *The Law of Attraction*, offers the idea of pivoting, which is finding the next best feeling or thought to enter our mind, the thoughts with less and less resistance. If you're feeling a big feeling, say, depressed about the church and what you went through, start there. Be in the depression.

The next best thought or feeling I could reach for might be rage. Why? Because rage feels better than depression. Being pissed about what happened lights a fire in me and gets me moving. And then, from there, the next best thought might be exasperation. Think eye-roll emoji. That annoyed feeling feels a bit better than rage, so I go there. And from an eye-roll, I might move toward the thought, "Well, thank God I'm not where I was." I move toward a feeling of slight gratitude. Why? Because gratitude feels a bit better than an annoyance. And then, from there, I might even be able to move to the thought of, "My life is way better than it was, and it's getting better all the time." Is that hope I hear?

There's no destination other than better. I might only get one thought away from the original, one degree closer to Peace than before. My friend, it is enough. You cannot jump from the depths of depression into the heights of Joy because there's no quick jump between them energetically. You can't just stop being pissed if you're pissed.

So, reach for the next best feeling or thought in moments like that. Be willing to reach for a new feeling because you care enough about how you feel to end your suffering, even just a little bit.

All of this is working on returning to Peace, the main and maybe the only goal. Peace has already become a regular part of the experience by this point in your practice. And as you discover how easy it is to return to your Peace, you also see how easy it is to springboard your whole experience into Joy by staying rooted in your Divine Self.

MANTRAS FOR LETTING THAT SHIT GO

I want to be happy more than I want to be right.
Who I am needs no defense.
The past is over, and it can touch me not.
I find shelter in my breath and find reasons to return to Peace.
I surrender the shit that's not working as often as I need to.

THINGS TO THINK ABOUT:

♦ Do I want to be right, or do I want to be happy?

♦ Who are the people with whom I need to feel right? Is there a shift that needs to happen?

♦ When I think about forgiveness, what comes up?

♦ Who still takes up space in my mind? Am I willing to let that go?

THINGS TO TRY:

1. Write a letter to that asshole who hurt you. Get it all out. Read it out loud. Then burn it.

2. Who is that one person who is living in your head, rent-free? Bring them to mind, and then say (if you can), "I love you, and I release you to the Holy Spirit." Or "I'm done with you, and I release you to the Universe." Or whatever variation of a release works for you. As often as they come up, release them. Notice how often they come up, and how it lessens over time.

3. Take stock of your practice so far. Have you seen an improvement in how you are feeling each day? In what ways?

4. Perform a chord-cutting ceremony. There's a million ways to do this, but here's the way I do it.

   a. Take two small candles, and with a sharp edge, carve your name into one and the other person's name into the other.

b. Set the candles in holders or affix them to a fireproof surface (like a plate) by melting the bottoms slightly with a flame.

c. Tie a string to each of these candles, and then light the candles.

d. As they burn down to the string and catch fire, separating the two candles, visualize the ties you've had in your mind to this person burning up, snapping, and dissolving into the flames. Watch as these candles of your connection burn down to nothing. Visualize the tension leaving your mind as the light shines from the flames.

e. As the candles burn down, take some time to journal and reflect on this connection and the glory of its release.

For extra fun, burn the letter you wrote in number one here.

5. Share with a trusted friend the work you've been doing. How has your life improved as you've kept your practices? As you've begun to let that shit go?

And listen to the immersive meditation on surrender and forgiveness at thekevingarcia.com/bloommeditations.

8 | THIS SHIT IS FUCKED UP

On Acceptance, Grief, and Joy

All that you touch,
You change.
All that you change
Changes you.
The only lasting truth
Is Change.
God
Is Change.

—Octavia Butler, *The Parable of the Sower*

Joy is not a choice that we make. I can't tell you the number of times I've heard the sentiment that you just gotta "choose Joy." They'd quote that verse that said sorrow may last the night, but Joy comes in the morning. It is the terrible propensity of western Christians to overlook the suffering of the cross in favor of the victory over death in Easter. We are not accustomed to tears. We are not able to handle grief. And we are all worse off for it.

People apologize for crying when they are sad. Isn't that bizarre? You ask how your friend feels when they've just lost someone to cancer, and they tear up and say, "Oh my god, sorry . . . " as if they didn't just have their heart shattered. Why do we do this?

Because grief isn't conducive to productivity. Productivity is all capitalism cares about. Your feelings are not convenient for your work schedule. If you are bogged down by your loved one's death, who will work your shift at the restaurant? Who is gonna take care of your kids? Who but you? A truly terrible conundrum we've found ourselves in, isn't it? Where we must compromise our well-being for the sake of keeping a roof over our heads.

Another misconception is the belief that we should always be joyful. We should always be happy and bubbly because of GOD! If we aren't experiencing the "Joy of the Lord" (what even is that?) all the time, then we must be doing something wrong. There must be something we aren't doing right, a secret sin or some malformation in our hearts. Just pray more. It should be fine.

And those people telling us to be joyful may have a lot of seeming Love and Joy in their life, but they are the least peaceful people I know. If their Joy gets interrupted, they are bent out of shape. If you've ever worked in the service industry, you know that the worst crowd and the cheapest cheapskates are the Sunday after-church crowd. The number of Christian tracts I received telling me that the biggest tip I could get was to get right with Jesus . . . I got enough that I had a burning ceremony at the end of each month to let that shit go. All that is to say I don't need to be taking advice on being joyful from people who have never walked through hell before.

Joy, like fruit, is seasonal. Sure, if we were enlightened beings, free from attachment, we would probably be experiencing the bliss of Divine union all the time. I am not like that. I assume that you probably aren't either. You and I live involved and integrated with this world. Being a monk in a cave tending a fire and talking to God away from the rest of society, à la the Desert Mothers and Fathers, sounds appealing for many reasons. But I'm also someone who loves going to gay bars and dancing and drag and sex and smoking weed. For better or worse, I plan to stay involved in the moves of my world.

And that means ups and downs. This means I am choosing the contrast. I am choosing to figure out what I want by running into things I don't want. I am accepting that part of the deal of living in and loving this world means I must experience contrast if I want to create something better. I do not have to like the shit that happens around me or to me or to my people, but I must learn to accept it.

LOVING WHAT IT IS

Octavia Butler said through her main character in *Parable of the Sower*, "God is change." It was the main idea of the character's faith and spiritual practice. She was living in a very dangerous, near-apocalyptic, near-future America. And she wrote the things she thought were obvious. This collection became known as *Earthseed: The Books of the Living*. In it, she posits that it is our duty as intelligent beings to shape the world as we want or suffer the consequences. Pretty clear and evident to me too.

Change is the only constant. The annoying little paradox that we don't contemplate enough. The only way to be at Peace is to be at ease in a world that grows, evolves, and changes. Resistance to change is the source of all suffering. We resist, most often, personal change. We are wrapped up in our own dramas and lives, fall in Love with our stories and stories about the people closest to us, and we often like it so much we don't want it to change. Or we try to shape each other into something more palatable to our liking. Or we try to shape ourselves into something unnatural to fit into a form more pleasing to those around us. Sometimes as a means of survival, and other times out of manipulation, but always out of a misguided perception that we should be something other than who and what we are.

Octavia says in a later *Earthseed* verse,

A victim of God may,
Through learning and adaption,
Become a partner of God,
A victim of God may,
Through forethought and planning,
Become a shaper of God.
Or a victim of God may,
Through shortsightedness and fear,
Remain God's victim,
God's plaything,
God's prey.

This makes God out to be a little more impersonal than maybe we are used to. If God is change, then God is indifferent in some ways. God is the power flowing through all creation, going hither and thither. This is why it's okay to rage at God. This is why it's okay to shake your fist at the creator of the Universe because at the end of the day, God is still gonna keep going. And if we feel we are victims of the world, we have two options:

Accept reality as it is or suffer more.

This doesn't mean I have to like it or even love it, but I would be happier if I learned to not beat myself up over having feelings about it. Acceptance is the process of coming to terms with what is. It's letting go of the sugarcoating, the platitudes meant to make us feel better, and sometimes giving up the comfort that takes us out of our suffering.

You ever just wanna feel mad? Or just feel sad? You wanna throw yourself a pity party? You should! You need to. As we learned in the last chapter, you gotta get that energy and sadness moving through you. Starting with what is, what reality is actually like, orients us toward the path. When we avoid the hard feelings, whatever they may be, they stay stagnant in the Body. Our energetic Body contracts and presses in on us, giving us a sense of being stifled or stuck.

And we're stuck because we were taught that our negative emotions are unacceptable. We operate from our capitalist training of "never let them see the whites of your eyes." Never let them see you crash. Never let them know you are weak because they will take advantage of you if they know. That's my thought process, at least.

But if I do not accept that I am furious, sad, disappointed, disgusted, whatever it is, I am doomed to stay there. Worse still, if I deny that I have these emotions, I am damned to hell in my own head.

When I say, "I need to accept reality," I am saying, "I see this suffering I am experiencing. And I recognize it as a moment of suffering. I will not try to bypass this. I will love my Body through this."

DEAD DAD CLUB

My dad and I didn't speak for three years, and then he died. I know, very awful way to begin a story.

That's how I remember it, and I can't go back and verify it with him now, but I have no reason to not trust my memory on this. I called him to come out to him as queer in the middle of the summer of 2015. We had a rough relationship up to then, and I wanted to connect with him. In that call, I apologized to him for putting distance between us. And I had. My ex-gay/conversion therapy training taught me that it was my father's fault I was gay. Because he didn't do his job as a godly father, I was reaping the consequences. I was being punished for my father's sins, apparently. And because of this, I resented him.

Not to mention, he was a super rough-around-the-edges guy with a lifetime of unresolved trauma from his early childhood and PTSD from military service during wartime. So it wasn't just that he was the reason I was gay. He was also not willing to do the work to help me.

Ex-gay therapy made me hate my father and idolize him as the source of so much influence on my life. I reasoned that the reason I struggled so much with my sexuality was that my connection with my father was nonexistent.

Anyway, I came out to him. I started calling more frequently, but he never really called me. I called him that Christmas when I went up to surprise mom after thinking I'd have to work through the holidays, and I've never felt a colder shoulder through an earpiece like I did when I spoke with my dad. You could hear the indifference and boredom, the "okay, when can I get off this call" tone. And so I got off the phone, wished him a merry Christmas, and said, "He will call me when he wants to."

He never called.

I'd get the occasional call from my brothers asking if dad and I had a fight, which is apparently what he said to them and everyone. So I laughed and realized he was even more delusional than I thought. He's just as mean as he was before. I don't need to change him. I just need to live my own life. He'll call me when he wants to.

Then around Christmas 2019, my boyfriend sat me down and said I need to call my mother. She got a call from my dad's second wife. "Your dad is going in for a biopsy tomorrow because he may have pancreatic cancer. We don't know for sure, but it seems pretty bad."

Once again, he didn't call me. The man got cancer and didn't call his child to tell them. He let his wife call his ex-wife to tell his child. Can you imagine the grief and flames that crept up the back of my neck, the tightness in my gut, the wail in my lungs that came rushing out at that moment, the pain needing to find expression through breaking anything I could find . . .

A week later, I was told he had stage four pancreatic cancer and was undergoing treatment immediately. Still no call. Four weeks later, I got a call that he was going into hospice care. Cancer spread quickly, and there was nothing to do but try to make him comfortable. Still no call. A week later, while packing my bag to the airport to see him, my brother called to tell me that our father had just died.

I stood there in the kitchen of a house that felt like a prison, and I couldn't believe that my father still didn't fucking call me.

Should I have called him? Should I have been the bigger person? Why didn't I just swallow my pride and learn to let go? Why couldn't I . . . why didn't I . . .

Because I couldn't. For whatever reason, I couldn't. Now life had changed. He was no longer in a Body, and I could no longer hold a grudge toward a physical person. That was painful to feel.

There was nowhere to put the rage and spite anymore. I had to hold it. There was no place to push the anger out too. It was all stuck now. And I realized it was never going anywhere. It was only ever doubling back on my soul.

My life fell apart again after that. My partner and I split up, and I moved twice. I was flat broke and trying to start divinity school, so of course, I did the only thing I could do: I bought myself a session with a badass astrologer who promised to help fill in the gaps for what was happening in my life.

I spoke with her on a rainy afternoon at the yoga studio where I worked. I'd sometimes show up early and work in the lobby because it was gorgeously aesthetically pleasing. As she worked through my chart, she immediately said, "Did someone in your life die recently?"

I couldn't say if it was just the energy I was giving off or if she saw it in my chart movements, but she knew I was grieving. "Who died?" I was shocked by her bluntness. That was the first question to shoot out of her mouth. And that wasn't the last revelatory thing she said. We went through the rest of the chart. We talked about how I was in the middle of my Saturn return (a period in which Saturn returns to its natal position and brings a lot of upheaval in one's life). I was learning what it was to be a teacher and a leader. But she honed in on the grief, the loss.

"You need to grieve." I knew she was right. I cried horribly ugly tears at my father's funeral, but it was mostly a sense of "I can't fucking believe they are making this guy out to be a goddam hero when he was such a failure of a man, such a failure of a father to me." I was so mad at him. I was so furious with his lack of presence, lack of care, lack of anything that resembled Love for me. And I was pissed that he died and I didn't get to show him how wrong he was.

I never got to show him how my life turned out to be magical. I never got to rub it in his face or have him show up to see just how happy I had become as an openly queer weirdo. I never got to prove him wrong. I never got to be correct. And it was devastating.

That was the day that I learned how to begin formally grieving.

She instructed me on how to create a simple grief altar for my dad (later in this chapter, I'll describe how to make one for yourself). It wasn't fancy. A candle. A photo of him from our summer vacations when our family was relatively young. And a letter I wrote and read to him.

I sobbed. I didn't say much, just wept because it hurt. And I was sad for a good long time. And sometimes, when I think about my dad, I still cry for everything I didn't get to show him.

Thankfully though, nothing lasts forever. Not even suffering. Not even death.

THE DEATH OF ILLUSION

Before I go on, I want to mention that this grief stuff isn't just for when someone dies. This is for when anything dies, hopes and dreams included. We get so attached to the ephemeral, so in Love with the vision of what we want life to be, that we have trouble enjoying this moment. We try to shape the world to make ourselves comfortable rather than shaping ourselves to move through the world with comfort.

Part of my work in healing was and still is grieving the life I didn't get to have. Being a devout evangelical Christian living in the American South and struggling with my queerness meant I missed out on a lot. I look back on some of it, and it just hurts.

I went to prom with Chelsea when I wanted to go with Scott.

I went to church functions instead of finding friends who would accept me for who I was.

I sang worship music instead of studying jazz because I was told it was more pleasing to God.

I didn't dare let myself get a boner near anyone lest I accidentally fall into bed with them, and I hated myself for not having more control over my urges.

Lots of unnecessary self-hate. So much wasted time that I'll never get back. It makes me furious if I fixate on it too much. Not to mention, on the other side of it, I look back at my past Self and wanna scream, "What the fuck is wrong with you? Why did you do that? Why didn't you leave sooner? Why didn't you start sooner?"

The answer is, "The world has fucked me up, and that's what's wrong with me. I did what I did because I was afraid of hell. I didn't leave because I was afraid of being alone. I didn't start sooner because I didn't know how."

Have you ever let You talk back to you? Have you ever let the part of you that you accuse, your past self, give you an answer? If you want to treat the world with compassion, you've got to start here. And trust me, you will feel better if you do.

You must forgive yourself for not knowing any better, for the things you think you did wrong, even if you didn't do anything wrong. You gotta realize that it's not your fault. Not all of it. Most of it, in fact, isn't your fault. You were lied to. But now you're awake. Now you look inside and see the path you've taken before and how it got you here.

And now you're willing to do something different.

OVER AND THROUGH

Like all the other shit in this book, Grieving is a practice. It's not something you do one time but something that becomes a part of your lifestyle. A grief practice allows you to normalize having feelings of all kinds, not just the permissible ones. And having grief be regular, and maybe even ritualized, helps us create the necessary space in our hearts through which to process all our fears, our sorrow, our angst, our anxiety, our anger, all of it. Grief makes the heart big enough to hold it all and dissolve it to perfection, compassion, and Love.

We don't grieve because we hate ourselves or the feeling. We do it because we love ourselves. Because we know, somehow, deep down, this shit is fucked up, and we don't know how to let go.

The thing is, there's nothing to let go of. As I said, these things move through us. And we must permit that movement to happen. We must let the soft animal of our Body feel whatever they feel, and if we promise to be with them through it, to stay conscious of the pain instead of getting lost in it, we can do something we never thought possible:

Heal.

One of my favorite prayers comes from a sci-fi book. In Frank Herbert's *Dune*, there is a group of cosmic space nuns called the

Bene Gesserit. Their details, while fascinating, are not important to my point. "The Litany Against Fear," which they recite in moments of extreme duress, danger, or threat of death, amazes me with its almost magical melting of my anxieties.

> *I must not fear.*
> *Fear is the mind-killer.*
> *Fear is the little death that brings complete obliteration.*
> *I will face my fear.*
> *I will permit it to pass over and through me.*
> *And when it has gone, I shall turn the inner eye to see its path.*
> *When it is gone, there will be nothing.*
> *Only I shall remain.*

Y'all need a minute to soak that in? 'Cause I do for sure.

The book's main character, Paul (the messiah figure), recites this to himself while he and his mother are trapped, spinning without control in a small aircraft, at the mercy of Dune's incalculably powerful sandstorms. They use this prayer to return them quickly to their right minds so they can discern if there is any way out, any means of survival they could quickly seize. And from their prayer, Paul gets the idea to fly above the storm and out to safety.

Now, in my daily life, I usually am not in immediate or life-threatening danger. Most of the time, my fears are of things not present. Most of the time, it's avoiding my fears that keeps them haunting me. And I'll mark any other unwanted feelings in that category as fear. I'm not feeling them because I'm afraid of them. Why? What am I afraid of? What would happen if I felt them? What's the worst possible thing that would happen if these emotions finally began to move through me?

I asked this of a client once, and they said, "Well, what if I never stop crying?" My love, your Body will eventually get exhausted, and you will pass out. You physically cannot cry forever. It's a fantastic feature of your beautiful Body. A hard reset is built in.

For what I need, I'd change the first line of "The Litany Against Fear" to "I am in fear." And I let that be a stand-in for whatever the emotion is. "I must not fear this emotion" is another great reframe.

I don't wanna say, "I must not fear." It's not a helpful statement for me. It's like when all those angels show up in the Bible and tell everyone, "Don't be afraid!" Even though you're a glowing being of light with a message from the literal creator of the Universe? And I bet you're armed? Or, if you are biblically accurate, you have like eight wings and forty-two eyeballs? What the fuck you mean "Don't be afraid"? I was literally napping, minding my own business, and now you're here telling me I gotta have God's baby? Or something of that nature?

Anyways, I love this prayer because it invites my Body to naturally move the emotional energy through me. And I am assured that on the other side, I will be okay. All of it will be gone. Only I will remain.

I was listening to an interview with author Elizabeth Gilbert. Her partner, Reyna, was dying of cancer. As Gilbert walked to the store to get some air, she looked up at the sky and said, "Okay, God, whatever you are trying to teach me, do it now because I don't want to have to learn this lesson again." I borrow this prayer as well.

I tell my Body the same thing. "Let's just fucking do this. Whatever you need, I'm here." And sometimes, that means I rage. Sometimes I stomp my feet up and down like a toddler. Sometimes I scream. And then sometimes those screams turn into sobs. And sometimes, the sobs subside into silence. But I am willing to feel the feelings because I will turn my inner eye to see their path when they are gone.

And the path leads me back to myself. It leads me back to equilibrium. It lets me get back to a level head so I can deal with everything else. It can be exhausting, and it requires us to have more space for our tender Self. We may feel sensitive, drained, and unable to bounce back at first. Just know that's precisely what is supposed to happen. This is where your Rest practice becomes paramount.

Resting and allowing yourself to be as tired as you are during grief begins an emotional and energetic composting process. In composting, scraps of our organic material, food scraps that aren't good for anything edible, are transformed into nutrients for our gardens. Things break down to bare essentials and are then used by plants to grow.

And pretty soon, among what was decaying, little green shoots appear. And this seemingly benign growth is the beginning of Joy.

NOTHING LASTS FOREVER

How long? How long is this going to take? That's the big question our Western minds want to answer. How long before I start to feel better? Or something different? How long before the pain goes away? How long before I feel Joy?

Well, what are you willing to do? Are you willing to let yourself have space to feel whatever it is you're feeling? Are you willing to take a nap? Are you willing to stay present and not numb out with wine or weed? Because if you are not willing to slow down long enough to squeeze out a tear or take a breath, you will struggle with it rather than just letting it flow through you like it wants to.

If you're working on the practices suggested in this book, beginning to form a daily spiritual practice that leads you to Peace, all of this work will be easy. You already know what to do because you do it every day. You must remain diligent in your practice when times are hard. I guarantee your devotion to your Body will help you more than you can possibly know.

The blessing of impermanence—that nothing lasts forever—is that grief also doesn't last forever. That alone is a spark of Joy that helps me move toward better. And that is the goal, isn't it? In all things, I'm trying to move with ease and toward ease. Toward Love. But if I'm not keeping my spiritual practices to make space for this vast ocean of emotion, if I don't open my heart wide enough for this stuff to flow over and through me, I will drown in it.

There's no shortcut for this shit. It takes as long as it takes. Funny enough, though, if you let go of your timeline and surrender your need to feel better, the pain gets processed faster. When I keep my heart open through my practices, I welcome it all, and in the wide-open spaces of my Spirit, it is all transformed by Love.

And it happens in waves. One minute you're good. The next, you're a blubbering mess. It happens immediately, and it happens years and years later. It doesn't matter. You're not asked to judge your emotions. You are invited to love them. You are asked to have compassion for everything you experience. That is how you transform it. That is how you heal from it.

Ram Dass said in a talk that when you lose someone to death, you should give yourself at least two years to grieve. And then, when you're done with that, grieve some more. When I think about my past and how I hid my true Self for the first twenty-five years of my life, I reckon I've got at least twenty-five years to heal from the shit I went through.

You have time to grieve, my love. Trust me.

The misconception is that our spiritual journey is supposed to be all sunshine. But everything is a cycle. Life and death. Day and night. Light and shadow. For everything, there is a season. For everything, a time under the heaven. You must learn to accept the seasons of life and move through them. Your willingness is everything here. It will be the thing to help you get through the dark night of the soul and see the dawn breaking.

And you'll see it first within the dark corners of your broken heart.

CREATING A GRIEF ALTAR

When someone in your life dies, set up a grief altar. It can be as elaborate or as simple as you like. The only firm suggestion I'll give you is that it needs to be in a place where you're going to see it every single day. Include a picture of your beloved dead, a glass of water, or something they enjoyed drinking, and if you're into crystals or any other symbols, add them.

Grief altars can be for folks you want to remain closer to or for those you need to find closure with after their death. For me, it started as the latter and ended as the former.

When you sit down with them, light a candle, take a deep breath, take a sip of whatever you're sharing with them, and then write a letter. Tell them what you need to tell them. Don't skip anything. And then read that letter out loud. Do not skip the reading it out loud part. Even if you feel stupid talking out loud to what seems like nobody. Do not stop if your emotions get caught in your throat. Even if you cry, especially if you cry, keep going.

I had a lot to say when I did this for my father. I told him I thought he was a bastard and an ass, and I felt he failed. I told him he fucked up. And when I said that out loud, I heard in my head, "I know." It felt like he was right there, sitting on the ground, next to me, owning his shit for the first time.

That made me even more furious at first. Now without a Body and all these worldly attachments, my dad suddenly has the humility to admit he was wrong?

Yes. Because everything that was keeping my father from loving me in life was now gone. If his spirit is still floating around, if he is still with me, he is free. And that means I can be too.

Leave your grief altar up for as long as it takes. When you see it in your house, take a minute to just breathe and be with the sorrow. If you cry, that's okay. Let it come, and let it move through you. Then thank your beloved for sticking close to you if that feels good. Remind yourself that they are still with you. You're just learning to love them without their Body. And that transition takes time. But remember, they live in your heart now. They live in your mind. They are closer now than they've ever been. You must direct all the Love you may have had for them in life into your Body because that's where they are.

My dad's grief altar evolved into my ofrenda, a type of ancestral altar kept by many Latinx folks to commemorate their dead. My grandparents and friends I've lost over the past years joined him. It is a site of healing where there was so much sorrow once. And it was giving myself the intentional space to grieve my loss that led me to eventual Joy.

There are moments every day that remind me of my loved ones who have died, who I still feel with me. We'll talk later about what I think happens after we die and the implications of believing in an afterlife or reincarnation, but suffice it to say that this one practice can be the starting point for healthfully processing death and the loss of loved ones.

BUT FOR REAL, HOW LONG WILL THIS TAKE?

I read a story in Sri Satchidananda's commentary on *The Yoga Sutras of Patanjali*:

Nārada, a great sage who lives in the heavenly realms and still walks among men, was walking along the road and encountered a man holding a complex yoga pose in deep meditation. As Nārada approached, the man opened his eyes and asked where Nārada was going.

"I'm going to heaven, Lord Shiva's house."

"Oh good," the meditating man responded, "Could you inquire as to how many more births I must take before I can cross the sea of samsara?" This means escaping the cycle of birth and death and being wholly liberated. Nārada agreed to ask the Lord and went along the road.

As Nārada went, he found another man dancing blissfully, chanting the names of God in ecstasy and Joy. The dancing man spotted Nārada and asked where he was going. Krishna responded the same way, and this man made the same request.

Nārada went to heaven, spoke to Lord Shiva, got the answers, and went back out walking. He came across the first man, still holding his pose. And he asked, "Did you ask Lord Shiva how many births I must take before I am liberated?"

"Yes," Nārada said, "Lord Shiva says you must take one hundred more births before you reach liberation from your Karma."

"One hundred more births?!" The man was incredulous and incredibly sorrowful. He'd had so many births already. He practiced for so long. He made his past ten lifetimes about the pursuit of God. He felt like he was so close to enlightenment and heaven, but still, he had one hundred births before he could let go. How could this be?

Nārada left the man, who was weeping by this point. He continued down the road and found the second man still dancing and chanting the names of God. He saw Nārada and asked him the same question.

"Lord Shiva says to look at the tree you are dancing under. Can you count the leaves on this tree?" The dancing man stopped for a moment and looked at the tree. It was huge. Easily tens of thousands of leaves. "You must take as many births as there are leaves on this tree to find liberation."

"That's all? Well, at least there is a finite amount. And at least it's not all the leaves of the forest. I know I will reach my goal eventually. Shall I count the leaves, Lord Nārada?"

Lord Shiva suddenly appeared in a fiery chariot and said to the man, "Come along! I'm taking you onto heaven!" Joyfully, the man danced his way all the way into Lord Shiva's chariot, and together they crossed the sea of samsara to heaven.

The second man's willingness had made the need for rebirth obsolete. In a moment of grace, his karmic wheel was broken. And in all moments where you are willing, your karma may be broken too.

The meaning is this: When you are willing to do what is needed to be free, freedom tends to show up faster. The first man couldn't bear the thought of suffering for another one hundred births. The second man was busy finding bliss and ease and didn't care if he needed more time. He was enjoying the journey, enjoying the practices, enjoying life on the way to whatever's next. He knew that the practices were made for him, not the other way around. The practices are made for us to taste the bliss available to us now, to realize that heaven is available now. To understand, in truth, we never left heaven at all.

You may encounter the same grief in different forms a thousand times. Welcome it. Rather than an attitude of "I should be over this by now," you can say, "I knew this would happen. It makes sense. I'm so glad I recognize this. I know what to do now."

Grief is probably the most demanding practice to maintain. But it is so powerful. It shows us how to be supremely compassionate to ourselves and lays the groundwork for new perspectives to spring forth when we finally surrender and turn the eye in to see the path that fear has taken.

Often, the path leads us back into Wonder. Our sorrow carves a path back to Love.

MANTRAS FOR GRIEF AND ALL THE OTHER STUFF YOU DON'T WANNA FEEL

I will face my fears, my grief, my pain, my anger, my sorrow, because of all of it belongs.

I will permit these wonderful emotions to pass over and through me.
I listen to my Body and I honor her/them/him.
Joy is on the horizon, on the other side of this dark night.
I will be as afraid as I need to be, and I'll still love my Body all the more.
This is a moment of suffering. I accept that it hurts. I will love myself harder.
Nothing lasts forever, except for Love.
This too will pass. And only I will remain.
All shall be well. And all manner of shit shall be well.

THINGS TO THINK ABOUT:

♦ When was the last time I cried?

♦ Do I fear my negative emotions?

♦ What do I think about life after death? Rebirth? How does this affect how I grieve?

♦ Is there anything in my life that I need to just fucking accept so I can get on with grieving it?

♦ What would it be like to clothe myself in unbearable compassion as I walk through all of this?

THINGS TO TRY:

1. Create a grief altar for your beloved dead as described in the above sections.

2. Spend some time in a graveyard. I know this sounds odd, but the stillness is so good for the soul. It normalizes the presence of our beloved dead and makes death a more normal part of our living experience.

3. When there's a public tragedy (i.e., a mass shooting, police brutality, etc.), write the names of those who died and light a candle, placing both on your altar. Spend time praying for the victims and their families, sending them your love. Do this as often as you need to stay tender to these heartbreaking events. Don't grow cold.

4. Memorialize dates and set time aside on those dates to remember, to grieve, and maybe even to fall apart. Mental health days are highly suggested on these days.

5. Write a letter to someone in your life who has died who you miss. What do you miss? What do you wish you could still have? How will you carry them with you as you continue down your path?

And listen to the immersive meditation on grief and acceptance at thekevingarcia.com/bloommeditations.

9 | THE SACRED EROTIC
On Pleasure, Wonder, and Love

If I speak in the tongues of humans and of angels but do not have love, I am a noisy gong or a clanging cymbal. And if I have prophetic powers and understand all mysteries and all knowledge and if I have all faith so as to remove mountains but do not have love, I am nothing. If I give away all my possessions and if I hand over my body so that I may boast but do not have love, I gain nothing.

—1 Corinthians 13:1–3, NRSV

When I heard that famous "love is" verse as a teen, I understood it immediately. I remembered that time when I was nine years old, giving my life to Jesus, feeling the sensation of pleasure and delight roll up in me like a hot spring geyser. I felt the truth clearly:

Love is all that matters for Love is all there is.

But this gushy, feminine sentiment was stifled by my church telling me how I should treat the soft animal of my Body. I learned to make it subject to my mind. I learned that my Body was a sinful and flawed device Satan used to wreak havoc on God's perfect plan. It was my duty to resist the schemes of the devil. Add on top of all that the special guilt and shame that one feels when their unspoken prayer requests at youth group were always about watching gay porn.

I felt so much shame about being who I was. The agony of desiring something that God abhorred was so great that I sought to end my life twice. Now here, on the other side of all that, after doing a lot of work, I realized that loving my Body is the only way to find liberation. I must go deep within to excavate all the lies that I have been fed over the years, the toxic beliefs that I hold still, even unconsciously. I must make room for Love within me.

Just as this universe is going on forever, I believe that there are infinite spaces we can explore within ourselves. There's always further down, there's always wider, there's always more. And as we explore this space within our heart space, the more expansive the space becomes, the more Love fills it. The experience of that Love is called Pleasure.

And yet for many of us, Pleasure was or maybe still is a four-letter word. It's taboo and nearly exclusively associated with sex. But pleasure is more than just sexual. Pleasure has many avatars: the feeling you get when you bite into something delicious, the Wonder that strikes you when you see the sunrise over the mountains, the ecstasy of a phenomenal orgasm, the quiet of desert spaces, the salt in your hair after coming out of the ocean, and the breath that you just took in. All of it can be an experience of pleasure if you are awake to it. Everything can become a moment of awe.

We have learned a backward lesson about Love, what it is to love others, and what it is to have unconditional Love for the world and ourselves. We think that Love is an action or a feeling. We believe Love is something we can grasp, when in reality, Love is so multifaced, incarnated in endless forms. We are trying to grasp an aspect of the unspeakable Goodness that holds this world and universe together.

We see Love as something to attain rather than something to experience. In its introduction, *A Course in Miracles* also says that we are not here to learn the meaning of Love, "for that is beyond what can be taught. It does aim, however, at removing the blocks to the awareness of love's presence, which is your natural inheritance. The opposite of love is fear, but what is all-encompassing can have no opposite." This has been my aim here in this book and the practices shared. Love has never gone anywhere. God doesn't need to show up anywhere because God never went anywhere. We are unaware that God is in this place, right Here, right Now. We are distracted by whatever it is that we get distracted by. We think this distraction is our nature. We think being pulled from God's presence is our default, our sin nature.

This is the issue and the underlying malfunction of most Western Christian systems: the belief that who you are at your very core, your essence, how you were made, is evil. Irredeemable. Toxic. Disgusting. To combat your inherent flaws and imperfections, you must layer virtue upon yourself. You must clothe yourself in righteousness through prescribed acts of goodness and piety. However, in Western culture, we learn that our abstinence from specific actions makes us holy, not the actions we take. And thus, we become the person who prays, thanking God that we aren't like those others, those sinners out there. It creates a narcissism that parades itself as humility.

Some folks call this the doctrine of original sin. We can trace it back. We know where it comes from, and yet, because the idea of humanity being inherently evil has been the pervasive thought and teaching in the West, not just in churches but in culture at large, it makes sense that to change your mind about this would take time. That thought has momentum. That belief has deep roots.

And what has the fruit been for you? Bitter, yeah?
Let me share with you something better.

Our siblings of Eastern faith systems see things from nearly the polar opposite perspective. Hindus, Jains, Buddhists, Yogis, some Orthodox Christians, and the majority of other faiths with their roots in the East start from understanding your Goodness. Your core, the seed of what makes you who you are, is Goodness. Is God. Is Love. Is pure creative force. The very center of your being is an endless ocean of God. Some call this your soul, and depending on your school of thought, it is either the deposit of Divinity in you that makes you long for union with it or the thing hidden within you that you must seek to realize that you are Divine. Either way, it starts by establishing the truth that you, at your core, are very, very good. And you're here with a purpose, the same purpose as God: to create beautiful things.

All of it. The emotions you have, even the "impermissible" ones, are good. The anger and the rage? Those are necessary. Your Body and the desires you carry, those are good. In fact, you need to learn to see your Self, your Body, and your desire as good things to remove your blocks to the awareness of Love's presence. You must undo the programming, everything from your past causing you to question your Goodness and whether your feelings are valid. Rather than needing salvation *from* your Body, you will find salvation *through* your Body.

By this, I mean that the means for finding Peace are within you, on the other side of your quieted breath and stilled thoughts. You desperately seek to run away from the feeling of shame and pain within, but as we've learned, when we let those feelings flow through us, we find freedom.

Sometimes the guilt and shame we've learned around our bodies keep us from pursuing the things that will give us life. We don't think we deserve to feel good. We don't think we should have pleasure. As stated, pleasure has become a four-letter word that only means sexual gratification. And while that is undoubtedly a part of it, we've got to seek a more extensive definition of pleasure that includes food, music, movement, art, nonsexual relationships, sex with your Self, and Rest. This will allow us to see the truth that we've always internally known:

God is the experience of everything.

HEDONISM VS. THE SACRED EROTIC

The false premise I had been living in for so long is that pleasure is always at someone else's expense. At the end of the day, someone is always on the losing end of the deal. We think pursuing pleasure means pursuing wealth and status as the capitalist empire defines them. We learn this by watching how the most powerful pursue their pleasure, which is almost always at the expense of others. For them to have so much, others must suffer or live with less dignity.

I do not think it is a sin to be rich. I think it is a sin to hoard riches while your employees suffer from not having enough, while some sleep on sidewalks, while there is a list of things one might do to alleviate pain with a small percentage of your wealth, and you do nothing. And by sin, I mean anything done or left undone that separates you from the awareness of Love's presence in some way.

In Oscar Wilde's *The Picture of Dorian Gray*, the main character, Dorian, is a wealthy socialite who commissions a painting of himself and then sells his soul in order to remain young and beautiful—as he appears in the painting—forever. Dorian devotes his life to the pursuit of pleasure, but soon realizes that as his appetite for the intense grows into lustful murder and the exploitation of others, the painting begins to look more and more gaunt. The worse Dorian acts, the older the painting appears. He goes to the far end of pleasure, without any balance or concern, just for the thrill, and the book ends with him unable to take the fact that he's stuck in arrested development. He faces no consequences, nothing and no one to tell him no. He falls into decadence, into hedonism, and eventually, the weight of his actions is too much. Spending hours staring at his painting, the image deteriorated to a skull and rotting flesh. He grows mad and stabs the picture.

The text says that a scream was heard in the house, and later people went in to find a painting of a handsome, young Dorian Gray stabbed through with a knife, while a pile of bones and dust lay on the ground.

This is an extreme story, but many of us were raised to think the pursuit of pleasure was just pure hedonism, an utterly empty pursuit that will leave us upset, broken, and alone while injuring multiple innocents along the way. We are taught that the purpose of pleasure, of any kind, is hedonism or will lead us to it. And yes, if your definition of pleasure is rooted in extremes, in only a vision of your small Self and how you can make your Body feel good no matter the cost, then yes, you've crossed into hedonism.

But how many of us, upon hearing the words "That hurts," wouldn't stop immediately? Most of us are not sadistic. The majority of us are not sociopaths. Rarely have I met a person with all their marbles that loved knowingly exploiting people. And even the super-rich have no idea how their lifestyle impacts others, not truly. If they came face-to-face with it, I wonder if it would change them. Anyone truly connected to Love cannot find pleasure in another's exploitation.

So if pleasure is not just about the sexual, the carnal, what is it about? What is pleasure? Can it be experienced without exploiting others?

Yes. I think so. From where I'm sitting, pleasure is exploring Love's presence within the Body, finding Joy and comfort and ecstasy in the physical manifestation we find ourselves in. Audre Lorde's essay, "Uses of the Erotic," says it perfectly: "The erotic is a measure between the beginnings of our sense of Self and the chaos of our strongest feelings. It is an internal sense of satisfaction to which, once we have experienced it, we know we can aspire. For having experienced the fullness of this depth of feeling and recognizing its power, in honour and self-respect we can require no less of ourselves."

Lorde is talking about a deep sense of knowing and feeling good that is so satisfying that once you taste and see how good it is to feel good, you could never go back. Your feet have touched the promised land, and you realize it was just beneath you the whole time. Going back to how it was before may enter your mind, but only for a second because you now have a goal, an aspiration that is truly worthy of your created Body. You finally understand that no one "deserves" pleasure. Life has nothing to do with deserving. It has to do with what you want. It has to do with your desire.

And I would call this an understanding of the sacred erotic: the deeply embodied knowledge of your worth, your desire, and capacity for experiencing the glory of life. The sacred erotic is stripping your embodied experience of any remaining shame, guilt, or self-condemnation. Where hedonism seeks to strip others of their autonomy and humanity, the sacred erotic centers those things and seeks the mutual benefit of anyone in its orbit. It is an embodiment of Love's nature of give and give, rather than give and take.

Wanting to feel good, wanting to feel pleasure for the sake of pleasure, is truly a wonderful experience. You can want something because you want it. Go deeper if you want to, but start with the fact that the craving exists. You are a creature who wants; specifically, your brain is hardwired to seek out good things and move away from bad ones. Your cravings may look different from your friends or community, and that's okay.

Pleasure is about finding out how good we can feel in all areas of our lives, and once we understand how good we can feel, once we witness how feelings of Goodness, of Joy, of pleasure can increase to untold levels, we settle for nothing less.

Only you can figure out what that "internal sense of satisfaction" feels like. Only you can define pleasure for yourself.

To me, it feels like deep breaths. It feels like ease. It feels like the touch of my lover's hand on my hip while we lay in bed. It sounds like *I Have Nothing* sung by a fat Black gay man at karaoke in the original key. It looks like strangers kissing on the dance floor and disappearing into that magical in-between space lovers go when they close their eyes. It tastes like pot roast and mashed potatoes that my friend made on a Sunday night after we shared a joint. Friendships make you laugh uncontrollably and remind you to not take your healing so seriously.

And yeah, sex is up in there too. I love hearing my lover or lovers moan because it's a (really fucking) good experience. But I also love the slight moan of satisfaction that happens when you take the first bite of an incredible dish. I love how sunrises and sunsets both make me breathless, reminding me that I'm on a rock floating through space, and God has seen it fit, once again, to let all eight billion of us go on. I love how my dog gives me kisses and I wonder how such a creature, so full of love, could love an asshole like me. I love how it feels to bang out six thousand words in a few hours. I love the sweat on my brow when lifting weights at the YMCA.

I want to marvel at everything. I stare at anything too long, I start to think about the fact that the atoms are choosing to stay together to keep the form, and I am amazed any of this is here. I stare at a tree for a moment and think about how it's breathing for me. This feels so good. And it leads me directly into Wonder, the state of gratitude and awe for this created world and how I participate in it.

WHEN I SAY WONDER

Wonder is one of my favorite concepts and ideas—one of my favorite words, honestly. It is synonymous with Mystery, Love, and God.

These feel so intertwined. And a feeling of awe feels like a natural result of Wonder. The desire to understand at its highest level is the desire to experience something without judgment, to let it shine, and to join with it. It reflects our desire for oneness. Wonder is brushing up against the perfection in whatever we are witnessing and, for a moment, realizing it exists within us.

That eternal longing for union is what I would call Love. It is the end of the search. It's the beginning of the creation of expansion. It is what we are here to do. It is who we are and what we are.

Interestingly, this eternal longing and satisfaction can only be felt here and now. It can only be understood in the Body when the mind joins it through stillness. Thích Nhất Hạnh said that when the mind is conscious of the in-breath and the out-breath, the mind and Body become one thing. And how often are they in the same place at the same time?

When I focus on my breath and think about all the things that have to happen with perfect execution for me to continue to have life continue in me, I am awestruck. I become grateful that my lungs know how to move the blood in and out of their cavities, that my blood knows how to suck the oxygen right out of the air and expel what it doesn't need. And that the carbon dioxide that floats out is used by the tree. And at the same time, the tree is eating sunlight, turning radiation into glucose and nutrients for itself and sucking up water and minerals from the dirt and turning it all into fruit or seeds. And then I consume what was once air, dirt, water, and fire, turning it all into a human. This human. This Body.

And you can tell me scientifically what's happening, but the fact that it happens at all is miraculous to me. You can say something changes into something else, and that still doesn't make sense to me. You can tell me how my lungs can suck the oxygen out of the air the same way a fish's gills suck the oxygen out of the water, and I will still not get it. You can tell me a plant absorbs sunlight and turns it into food; I will never grasp how it actually *does* it.

Divine intelligence. Down to the atomic level and out to the furthest reaches of the expanding Universe. That is what I'm talking about when I mean Wonder. That is what I mean when I talk about being in Love. And with that kind of perspective, how could you not fall headlong into the sheer Joy of it? How could you not delight in it? How could you not find pleasure?

From where I'm sitting, the experience of pleasure, to be in Wonder and awe about this embodied experience, is to be aware of Love's presence. And by this point in our spiritual practice, by the time we have all the other ideas and principles working, this one becomes nearly effortless. It is an exclamation point on the end of declaration of freedom. It is the natural result of your practice.

One thing that helped me really embody this idea was finally realizing where God was. Before, when I prayed I was praying to a distant sky daddy somewhere else, begging for attention with so many words and actions and songs and dancing. Now, I realize the location of God is actually in the subtle pulse of my heart pushing blood through my Body. Now, I can hear God breathe when my lungs inflate. Now, I can feel God hold me when I hold myself.

Said another way: a practice of pleasure, of centering your good feelings, of practicing things that make you come alive, will allow you to become enraptured by the world and become a student of Wonder. And when you are a student of Wonder, you can experience Love in everything. And as you experience Love in everything, you will finally care enough about how you feel to end the suffering in your life.

THE END OF SUFFERING

This is where we are headed. To the end of suffering. To the center of Love's heart. Into the body of the Mystery. And what I've shared with you is an approach to becoming more one, more whole, more okay. But know that it is not the only way. In fact, this might work for you at first for a time, and then as you grow and change, you will need something different.

However, I caution you about raw dogging life without some kind of baseline of practice. What I mean by that is, don't do the buffet line thing. Don't just go into your spiritual life picking what looks good, overloading your plate so much that you can't enjoy the meal. So many of us think, "Oh, let me just do this on my own. I'll pick and choose from all these various traditions and see what feels good." And then, as we get addicted to feeling good, we also use all the new fancy language, but in reality, we're stuck in the same traps. Then we get mad at ourselves because we think there's something wrong with us for not "doing better."

My advice to you: Stick with this practice for a while. A good while. Dig this well deep enough to strike water, and then you will not need to dig all these tiny holes everywhere, disappointed you can't find the living water. You must find pleasure in the little things, name them as good, and keep track of them. You must intentionally lean into practices that guide you back into Peace, and stay there long enough to experience the benefit.

You might need to see a therapist while creating your spiritual practice. You might need to talk to a psychiatrist about medication to help. I've been on meds to help manage my anxiety and depression for over five years, and I don't imagine a time when I will be off these meds. They have saved my entire life and helped me so much. They level the playing field so I can engage with all the stuff I've discussed in this book.

Regardless of your mental health, your practice, or whatever else you think you lack, if you get nothing else from the words in this book, I need you to get this:

You are Wonder, fully made.
There is no separation between You and Love.
Suffering is a part of the experience here, and there's a way out.

And I offer this all to you in hopes that you will find your way back to your heart, to the Love within, to the Source undisturbed and incorruptible. I offer these practices and meditations with the assurance that those who are ready will implement them and find a way back into the flow of what God is already doing. I give this book to the world as a way to show my Self the path I must take and remind myself that I will always be a student and devotee to Life.

You who read this, I pray my blessings upon you, the blessings of my brother, teacher, and friend, Jesus. May you know the presence of Love deeply within your Body. May you feel the guidance and Wisdom of your right mind, your stilled breath, and your ancestors who are still with you. May you remember what Peace feels like and return to it as often as you fall away. May you remember nothing lasts forever, not even suffering or death. May you be in Love.

MANTRAS FOR LEANING INTO WONDER

I am God's Wonder, fully made.
Through the erotic, I find how far God's pleasure can take me.
I am the endlessly knowable Mystery.
When I breathe, the earth breathes with me.
I open myself to Love's presence now.

THINGS TO THINK ABOUT:

♦ What's my relationship to my Body? To pleasure?

♦ What things inspire a sense of Wonder in me?

♦ What stories have I been told about pleasure? About feeling good?

♦ What does this statement feel like to you? "The will of God is but my own."

♦ When do I feel most aware of Love's presence?

THINGS TO TRY:

1. Get fully involved with your meal. Cook yourself something or go to a restaurant you've been dying to go to. Put your phone on Do Not Disturb and be present. Relish each bite, chewing it at least twenty-one times.

2. Go dancing somewhere. Either at a club or a movement workshop or an ecstatic dance gathering. Or put in your headphones and dance in your house. Get your Body moving. Doesn't matter how. Just let the music move you.

3. Sit next to a tree. Lay your back against it. Close your eyes and breathe. Think about how you and this creature are breathing for one another.

4. Look at your naked Body in the mirror and tell your Body, "I love you. As you are. For what you are. For all you will become." Say it out loud. What does this feel like?

5. Go shopping for a new outfit. Cut your hair. Wear the makeup. Get the chest binder. Pierce your ears. Get a tattoo. Do something to claim stewardship and Love of your magical Body. Something they say you can't or shouldn't do that you've always wanted to do.

And listen to the immersive guided meditation on Wonder, pleasure, and Love at thekevingarcia.com/bloommeditations.

10 | A LIVING PRACTICE

I won't pretend I'm a big deal. This gift is a big deal.
The force behind the gift is who I serve, that's the big
deal. And I get to express how major the big deal that is
within me.

—Toni Jones, *I See Thoughts*

Thank you for making it this far with me. I've been talking about
many concepts and theories throughout this book. I've given you
some theology and new ideas that hopefully have begun to sprout
and root in you. And maybe you've gotten all the way to the
end of this book, tried some stuff, and still aren't feeling better
than you did at the start. Maybe this book and the practices have
brought up a lot of unprocessed pain you are now dealing with.
Perhaps you finally see how you can escape your suffering, but
still feel like you can't.

I want you to hear this clearly: There's nowhere to get to.
There's nothing to heal. There's no more to become. And on top
of that, you'll never get this shit done. You'll likely never be able
to transcend your bodily experience and enter into pure bliss,
statistically speaking. But my love, from the small taste you get in
Living Practice, do you not see that you've found heaven?

So take a breather. Your purpose is not to heal but to enjoy this life. To enjoy the process of cocreation with all of life. To have fun. To expand. Some of it will be painful, but you know that. Contrast is part of the process. You run into things that will cause you to freak out and say, "UGH, NO, NOT THAT." And then, reflexively, you will also know what you want.

Life is not a mountain-top experience forever. The air is too thin up there. Most of your life is gonna happen on the road. Sometimes the road is paved, but other times you'll find thorns and rocks. Count on running into them. And count on you leaning into your practices every step of the way. Count on you having a deep connection to Love and times when you feel lost in a dry, dry desert. Not if, just when. And when it comes, you can smile and say, "I knew this would happen."

Because you did. When you came into this form, when you took birth, you did so with the knowledge that everything you'd experience here would spur you toward your most creative potential. You knew that there would be things that would come to you to be tested, not to test you. To see what would be worthy of your experience and what would go on. You must realize that this is all part of the delightful process of creation.

But how do we stay there? How do we, as much as possible, remain in that deep connection to God? To All? To Self? To the Universe? To Love?

We do so by developing a Living Practice, a sustainable spiritual practice that is marked by the presence of the fruit of the Spirit. We start with Practice. We practice a restful approach to life. We are willing to do these things because they bring out the best and make us feel fantastic. As we begin to feel good about who and what we are, we find the people who help us maintain that feeling, help us shine, and cause us to bloom. In these spaces, we learn to speak with radical honesty, and in making plain what we feel, need, and want, our boundaries naturally occur. We surrender all that would break our hearts to Spirit. We accept who and what we are, as well as what is. We find Pleasure in it.

Simple as that.

Okay yeah, but how? How do I do this?

So glad you asked.

DEVELOPING A LIVING PRACTICE

This will be the clear, point-by-point how-to for creating a Living Practice for yourself. We all can and should customize our Practice. The only thing I ask of you, whatever you do, is that you must be consistent. In the West, especially those of us who come from Religious Trauma Land, we have a terrible habit of not sticking to something that doesn't have instant results.

Some feelings will come up at first. At first, your Practice might give you access to deep places within you, and this can be thrilling. The opposite might also be true. It might be so freaking uncomfortable at first that you are weary of continuing your Practice. No matter where you land, I'm gonna ask you to trust me. Follow my instructions here. Practice in earnest, and in the next thirty days, you will have developed a solid practice that will need nothing but your breath to guide you.

So, let's do it!

Question first: What did they tell us to do to become stronger Christians and strengthen our faith? It was three things:

Read your Bible.
Pray.
Go to church.

How were we so good at that? For a long time, I followed this pattern and felt some sincere feelings. I was better than all my friends at all of this, and at the same time I was afraid to not do them. I was scared that if I didn't keep these practices, I would more easily fall into sin. I had to track all my thoughts and make them captive, obedient to God. I needed to read God's word. I needed to hang out with God's people. It was just . . . the thing.

But over time, keeping these things out of a rote of responsibility left me feeling dead inside. They were dry. The words of my Bible triggered me. I was trying to pray to God and hearing nothing but the silent void in answer. Going to a church building only to have the pastor talk shit about me and all my queer friends made me feel terrible.

Truth be told, though, those practices we had were solid. But no one really taught us how to read our Bibles. No one taught us critical thinking or about the poetry of it or the more profound Wisdom in it. We learned it was "basic instructions before leaving earth." Same thing with praying. It's a good thing, but we were not taught what it was for or could do it for us. And the people we gathered with were just as brainwashed and bamboozled as you and I were.

As I started to explore a regular spiritual practice on my own, I ironically and inadvertently stuck to what worked before, but I tweaked it all. I updated the modality and chose the deeper Practice in each of these prescriptions.

Rather than reading my Bible, I began reading inspiring texts of all varieties. Poetry. Holy texts of other faith traditions. Essays by womanist theologians. Writings of early Christians from before the canonization of the Bible. Gospels that were kept out of the canon. New age and metaphysical texts. I no longer feared getting tempted or deceived because I wasn't looking for what was true. I was looking for what was helpful.

Instead of praying to white Jesus and asking daddy God to forgive me for thinking about men and sex like an average human with a sex drive, I began getting quiet. I started learning about breath work and meditation, and at first, I used the Headspace app to teach me the basics of watching my thoughts and my breath. The variety of meditation techniques and ideas was so beautiful and astounding. It showed me that meditation was a more effective path to connecting with the Source I wanted to be with. It was not about getting rid of anything but remembering what Peace felt like. To remind me of Love's presence in all things. Doing this regularly changed my fucking life.

And because I did not feel like getting up for church, not even for a dope, queer-affirming, progressive congregation, I had to figure out a regular time to get together with my friends. I needed to be with people I could air all my bullshit to, people I could complain to, and folks to remind me of when I was getting too much on my bullshit. I wanted people with whom I could delve into the deep topics of life, the spiritual aspects of things, and who helped me come alive.

Finding inspiring texts, daily meditation, and regular gathering became the foundations of my Living Practice.

If you are starting from scratch and need clear instructions on building this out for yourself, try the following prescribed Practice for at least twenty-one days.

INSTRUCTIONS FOR BUILDING YOUR LIVING PRACTICE

Week 1

Every day, at the top of your day before you get to work or any of your daily tasks, take five minutes for yourself.

1. The first minute should be a little stretching of your Body. You don't need to do sun salutations from yoga or Thai chi. Just move to wake up your Body.

2. Then read a selection from a text that inspires you. If you need some suggested readings that I've loved, check out the list at the end of this chapter.

3. Find a phrase that stands out to you in the text that sums it up. Nothing too long. Use this as a mantra as you meditate.

4. For one minute, focusing on your in and out breath, repeat the mantra in your head. When you find your mind has wandered, gently return to the mantra and the breath.

5. After that minute, take a moment to write down what came up in that time. What did you feel? Affirm that you wish to take this feeling of Peace with you throughout your day.

Do these things by your altar or meditation space that you've set up. (See the end of chapter 2 for more information on creating an altar space.)

As an added fun practice, set your alarm for 9 a.m., 12 p.m., 3 p.m., 6 p.m., and 9 p.m. When the alarm goes off, take one minute to practice a breath meditation. Remember your mantra for the day. Check in with your Body. What do they need right now? What can you do to return to Peace at this moment?

Do this for one week. Do not attempt more than one minute of meditation right now. Let yourself be easy with this. And do not push yourself to have a longer practice right now. Too many of us push ourselves because we think we should be good at having a thirty-minute silent, seated Practice, and we burn out because we can't do it. Of course you can't do it yet. You're still learning to regulate your inner world.

Week 2

You're going to double everything. This may take eight to ten minutes, depending on your reading and how long journaling takes.

1. Move and wake up your Body for two minutes.

2. Read the selection from the text that inspires you. Find your mantra.

3. Meditate on this mantra for two minutes.

4. Write down in your journal what you experienced in meditation. Takeaways. Things you want to remember. And affirm that you want to take this feeling with you all day.

5. At the same time intervals as before, and when the bell rings at those times, stop for two minutes. Set a timer, close your eyes, and breathe.

Do this for one week. Do not attempt more than two minutes of meditation right now. If you're struggling to keep up with these practices by the end of this week, do not move on. Repeat this specific Practice until it becomes comfortable and easy for you. Then, when you are ready, continue.

Week 3

Double everything again. Depending on how much you're reading, this may take twelve to fifteen minutes. However, if last week felt challenging, repeat the Practice of week 2.

1. Move for four to five minutes to wake your Body up. If it feels good, follow a yoga sequence of basic sun salutations. Make sure you drink some water too.

2. Read the selection from the text that inspires you. Find your mantra.

3. Meditate on your mantra for four to five minutes. When you find your mind has wandered, go back to your mantra and breath.

4. Write in your journal what you experienced.

5. At the same intervals as before, if you can take five minutes, do so. If your life disallows you from taking five minutes at these intervals, take one to two minutes or whatever you can. Even if you just hear the bell and remember to breathe deeply, that will be more helpful than nothing.

Do this for one week. Do not attempt more than five minutes of meditation.

Week 4

Evaluate your Practice.

What's working for you? What felt really good? What made you feel deeply connected to Source? What didn't feel comfortable? What came up for you now that you are ready to heal? And the best question is, Do you want to keep doing this? Does this make you bloom and come alive? Does this connect you with your Divine Self? Does this inspire you and make you wanna go deeper?

Remember, this is a starting place. I've got plenty of thoughts about what comes next. But none of that will be beneficial if you cannot commit to something like this. For some folks, feeling better, feeling Peace, and surviving late-stage capitalism with a modicum of sanity is enough for them. For others, you're not going to be satisfied with just feeling baseline okay. You're gonna want to go deeper into Love. You're gonna want to delve into the mysteries of it all, to not just touch the Source but to merge with it. To let Love and You, the Beloved and You, merge.

This is a lifelong Practice. This is the point of being here, on this particular earth. I'm not going to tell you it will take a lifetime. Every time we get a taste of Peace, we are there. And then we come back to earth and our desires and all that stuff, and then we go back to God. It's a cycle. And I'm okay with not being spiritually high all the time. Sometimes life is boring. Sometimes the Practice is rote. Sometimes it becomes stale. It's then up to me to make it fresh again. I need to not let my inner world become dusty. And frankly, I don't know anyone with a spiritual practice who would describe their inner world as boring.

FINDING INSPIRING TEXTS

The Bible isn't the word of God. I don't know if you knew that, but it is not. It's just words about God. And so are all the other holy texts of the world. So is poetry. So are essays. So are song lyrics. So are scripts and plays. So is your life.

If holy texts are not your cup of tea right now, if the Bible is still a trigger point for you, don't go there. Let it go for a while. Work on healing, becoming whole, and being able to be your own spiritual authority before you return to anything weaponized against you. When you are finally grounded and connected to Love, you'll be able to approach any text, discern the Wisdom within, and leave the rest.

Some texts I would suggest you check out:

A Course in Miracles: A metaphysical text that takes Jesus Christ's teachings to the Nth degree. It allowed me to undo much of my fear of God and has a workbook for students to apply the instructions.

The Gleanings of Bahá'u'lláh: A small selection of sayings from the prophet of the Bahá'í faith. I found his words inspiring and reflective of one who has known God.

Be Here Now: Ram Dass's first big contribution to the spirituality and consciousness conversation. It was written when he was relatively young in his journey, but the text is still gorgeous, full of pictures and weird formatting. And it's a gorgeous piece of work.

The Yoga Sutras of Patanjali: As translated with commentary by Sri Swami Satchidananda. While this text is aimed at celibate men seeking to be monks within yogic traditions hundreds of years ago, this text holds the Wisdom of what regular Practice gives us. Satchidananda's commentary is rich, and his storytelling is so wonderful.

The New New Testament: An edited and updated edition of the New Testament with curation by Dr. Hal Taussig. This includes many of the gospels, poetry, and letters that were important to early Jesus peoples before the movement was co-opted by the "Holy" Roman Empire.

The Artist's Way: Julia Cameron's work on creative living as a spiritual path has enhanced the lives of countless folks. While not explicitly a metaphysical text, it is deeply spiritual and an incredibly hands-on approach to spirituality.

Sister Outsider: Essays by Black womanist Audre Lorde. Her conception of Pleasure and the erotic and her intersectional work of justice give me a picture of what it could be like to find heaven in my Body.

Rest Is Resistance: A manifesto on how Rest will save us all by Tricia Hersey. As I said before, nearly everything I know and practice around the idea of Rest is derived from following her example.

Meditations: Selected poetry from Mary Oliver. Are you even a mystic if you haven't read Mary Oliver's words? She provides such beautiful words to describe the human experience.

Meditations on the Tarot: A translated text by an anonymous French monk on how the tarot shows us a path back to God.

When Things Fall Apart: American Buddhist monk Pema Chödrön gives an excellent discourse on what to do when your life, your faith, or You just fall apart. A must-read for folks learning to grieve.

Inner Engineering and *Karma:* Sadhguru is a living Indian mystic and saint. His works and teaching are prolific in the modern yogic discourse and spiritual movements. He's someone I revere quite a bit.

The Parable of the Sower and *The Parable of the Talents:* In her last two works, the way the incomparable Octavia E. Butler's Afrofuturistic mind painted the rise of Christian nationalism almost exactly as it has happened in our modern day is horrifyingly poignant. Her writings on faith and belief within this text are unparalleled.

The Essential Rumi and *The Soul of Rumi:* Translated and edited by Coleman Barks. Rumi's words as a Sufi and Muslim mystic have inspired countless folks, and his words go right for the heart of the heart, cutting through our resistance and ushering us into Love's presence.

PRAYER AND MEDITATION

Meditation has replaced my former definitions of prayer. When I was younger, I was told we needed to pray to talk to God. And yet I was always confused about how God was supposed to talk back to us. It was always so mysterious.

Prayer now is anytime I am naming that which is deepest within me. Both the Joy and the most profound sorrow. It is asking the Universe to help, asking my saints, angels, ancestors, and God to help me find and get what I need. But it is also a way for me to recenter. I recognize that while I have many problems, I really only have one: I sometimes believe I'm separate from God.

Meditation is the time that reminds me I am not separate from but one with God, with Love. It is when I let the wild thoughts that fly around my head—my fears and projections—subside for a moment so that I can remember what Peace feels like. I come back to my clear, still mind. I let ego and fear pass through me so that I may hear Wisdom again.

I do this daily. I do this often. I do this not to make me holy but because I need to be reminded that my Holiness is who I am, that my Holiness blesses the world, and that there is nothing my Holiness cannot do.

Doing this alone feels so good. Now imagine doing this with others. Imagine a whole group of people waking up and getting in touch with the same Source of Love you are. This is who you should gather with.

The question "How often should I do this? How long should I sit in meditation?" comes up. My teacher responded to the same question I had with, "Well, how often should you brush your teeth in order to not get cavities?" This isn't a good or bad thing, an issue of holiness or separation. The presence of cavities means that you've neglected yourself in a specific way. The same is true of the soul and Body. If you're experiencing some rot of the soul, it's because you have not attended to it with what you know could help heal and prevent further infection. Don't meditate because you think you must. That is religion. Do it because you know it will set you free. That is a living practice.

For the average person, even just five minutes at the top of the day can give you access to Spirit, to that awareness of Love in all things. I'd say that ten minutes is better. For someone who may consider themselves a spiritual seeker, twenty minutes minimum should be your aim. And for those among us who consider ourselves teachers, your entire life should be built around your practice. An hour of movement, writing and reflecting, chanting perhaps, and stillness will keep you in a place where you can actually care for the people you are charged with leading.

Again, meditating for longer, having more elaborate spiritual practices, etc., none of it makes you better. Not meditating or having a simple, short, and sweet practice does not make you a worse spiritual seeker. We all have different needs and desires. You just must ask, "What do I want?"

GATHERING REGULARLY

This is the most experimental part of what I'm talking about because this is the thing we're missing the most. The data tells us that the number one thing people miss when they leave the church is community. We miss having people who we can call our friends. Church allowed a lot of us to have everything above built in. And it also feels scary because we fear it might be more of the same. What if people are just as fake? What if I get triggered?

Beloved, what if you stay where you are? What if you remain lonely? Then what?

Octavia Butler says in her writing of *Earthseed: The Books of the Living*, verse 27:

> *Once or twice*
> *each week*
> *A Gathering of Earthseed*
> *is a good and necessary thing.*
> *It vents emotion, then*
> *quiets the mind.*

It focuses attention,
strengthens purpose, and
unifies people.

I could not agree more. But we have to do it differently. When I was still dedicated to the church, we often talked about the table being central, meaning the communion table. The eucharist ritual symbolized the supreme equity between all persons because all of us were offered bread and wine by the same Lord. As I came out and fought for a spot to belong in church, I often remarked that Christ set the table, and we are all welcome. I would fight to be in places that didn't want me because I deserved respect.

And yes, I did deserve that. But why would I want to brutalize myself? Why would I fight for a place at a table that would not even acknowledge me even if I was spitting in their food? I don't want to fight for a place anywhere. I know that I belong. And another person's choice to love me or not can't delay me any longer.

A few years back, when I started dreaming about a new spiritual community, I heard the song "Crowded Table" by The Highwomen. And it perfectly spelled out what I wanted in a spiritual community, in my group of friends that I would do life with. The chorus says, "I want a house with a crowded table and a place by the fire for everyone. Let us take on the world while we're young and able, and bring us back together when the day is done."

So simple. So perfect. And so clear. This is what I endeavor to do when I curate spaces. I want it to feel like you can sit with us no matter how different we are. You can rest with us. You can dream with us. You can heal with us. And while we could just freewheel it, I believe we are coming together for a purpose. It doesn't have to be strict, but a structure is helpful for creative forces to be concentrated and used in a way accessible to everyone present.

If you want to start gathering people around you at a crowded table, living room, yoga studio, backyard, forest cabin, or wherever you choose to gather, I suggest the following structure.

LEADING A GATHERING

1. Whoever is curating the space should welcome people to the space. You do not have to be formal if it's just people you know. But if you have new folks, make them feel at home.

2. Explain the flow of what you'll be doing that evening. "We'll start with reading a text from _____, and then _____ will lead us in meditation, and then _____ will share their heart tonight."

3. Choose someone to read a selected text, either something that you've found inspiring, a theme the guided meditation will focus on, or a text that the person speaking will be centering on. Ideally, the curator has already lined these things up ahead of time.

4. Choose someone to lead the group in a guided meditative experience. If no one can do this, listen to a guided meditation together.

5. After meditation, choose someone to share their heart. This can be a homily, a dharma talk, the poetry they've written, a mini-sermon, or a TED talk-style sharing.

The elevation and edification of all present should be the point.

6. After the person has concluded their talk, hold a moment of silence, and the curator will invite those present to question the person who spoke. They may ask questions for clarification, take concepts further, and even push back on what was shared. Every person who speaks should be ready to be questioned.

7. The formal part of the gathering should end in prayer for the community and blessing for those present.

8. Share a meal together. It would be wise for your meals to be potluck-style and/or to have vegetarian and vegan options so many people may participate.

Regarding when to gather, most faith communities gather once a week. That seems to work for a lot of people. If that feels good to the group, y'all should do that. Another option might be following the cycles of the moon. Gathering on the new and full moon is a beautiful, cyclical choice. And if you're an astrology goon like me, you can easily fold in themes and ideas from the astro-weather. And if you wanna get a little witchy, you can start following the pagan Wheel of the Year, which observes the changing of the seasons, the equinoxes, the solstices, and the midway points between the four major seasons. If you're like me, you'll involve everything you've picked up along the way. You'll integrate what is helpful with deep reverence for the tradition it originated in and bring it with you on your journey. You'll find what makes you bloom and what tastes like Love.

AN ALTERNATIVE LIFESTYLE

To taste the fruit of Love, there is nothing you need to do, but there is everything you need to be. Like everything else, it is an experience you have due to a process.

If you have spent time in your spiritual practices, your Self-Control has likely increased because you understand that Self-Control is not a matter of deprivation but a matter of Gentleness and ease. The feeling of ease you've created results in Faithfulness to practices. And as you are compassionate and gentle with your Self, it is easy to be generous with others in every manner. If you are generous, you can't help but exhibit Kindness. And kind folks are nearly always patient. And because they are, they experience Peace, revel in Joy, and stay rooted in Love.

I shared at the beginning of this journey that this is just as much mysticism as it is mathematics. And I'll also remind you of this: while bad theology will kill you, good theology won't save you. Meaning it isn't enough just to believe the right things. If you want to feel better, beloved, you must shift your lifestyle.

And dare I say, by picking up this book, you *are* trying to live an alternative lifestyle. A lifestyle that isn't based on the capitalist need to own and produce but rather one whose hallmark is Love, Joy, Peace, Patience, Kindness, Generosity, Faithfulness, Gentleness, and Self-Control. I'd also dare to say that pursuing this path is way easier than pursuing what much of Western society seems to value. It may feel like you are incapable of breaking out of the patterns you've been in for so long, but remember: it is not difficult. It is merely different. And making that change of mind is essential in allowing these new ideas to take root.

Nothing about this process is hard to grasp. It is opposed to the way you've been living for so long, and when you begin to get aligned with Love, when you stop tolerating living small, when you create boundaries, when you start to get your needs met, those who have known you only as who you were before will try to treat you as they did before. And you will notice that you have a lower tolerance for things that are anything less than loving, anything less than Peace.

The motivation for all this is that I want to feel good. I want to come alive. I want to feel that I am God's Wonder, fully made. Because when I am in the center of that, I feel my best. That is it. I keep my practices so I can enjoy my life. I've said before that I'm not trying to transcend anything. I'm not trying to escape this Body or this world. I am attempting to love them both entirely as part of my Self.

And that is way easier than loathing everything.

As you finish up this book, I want you to check in. How are you feeling now versus when you began reading this book? Did you engage with the practices at all? Were they helpful? Did you just read the words and get some good ideas, and maybe you're getting ready to dip your toes in? Wherever you are, whatever you are feeling, I want you to know that I love you.

I love you. You don't need to perfect anything. You don't need to master shit. You are enough. You are good. You are lovely. You are powerful. You are able. You are self-controlled. You are gentle. You are faithful. You are generous. You are kind. You are Peace. You are Joy. You are Love.

I pray that you begin your Practice, small and mighty. That you devote yourself to your Peace, to your healing, to the people who make you bloom, and to a lifestyle that grows your faith into a garden so abundant that others may take Joy in the beauty you create.

If you take nothing else from this book, if you take nothing else from this offering, please, please, please tattoo this upon your heart:

You are God's Wonder, fully made.

And you don't have to believe that.

However, you'd be unspeakably happy if you did.

ACKNOWLEDGMENTS

I've been a community-made creative from the very start of my career. I am so grateful to you, dear reader, for lending your support, prayer, energy, and Kindness to me as I seek to live out a vocation that still feels a bit hazy at times. I love you.

I'd like to name a few folks specifically for helping me get to where I am and helping bring *What Makes You Bloom* into full blossom:

David Morris, you're the best agent a gal could ask for.

Lisa Kloskin, you're an author's dream editor.

David Harshada Wagner, my teacher and mentor, I'm so grateful to you and how you help me go deeper into the heart of Love.

Tricia Hersey, the Nap Bishop. I know we've never met, but your words have saved my Body and soul. Thank you for teaching me what you know about dignity and divesting from capitalist schemes. I know it came at a price.

Rev. Dr. Keith Menhinick, for late nights in the kitchen as I hashed out these ideas, bouncing them off you, and laughing a ton as we went. You're such a fun conspirator.

Dr. Christena Cleveland, for giving me the privilege of going second. You doing you, chasing your devotion to the Black Madonna showed me the devotion I can have in my own life. Your example changed me. Thank you.

Rev. Dr. Jacqui Lewis, for the support, encouragement, and words of inspiration. My work wouldn't exist without seeing how you show up in this world as your full, radically loving Self. Thank you.

Matthias Roberts, I just think it's really cool that we're living our dreams now. Ain't that wild? Once again, you being my friend has helped me to keep doing the work and reminded me why I do this work. Love you.

The Promise Breakers, Tim, Chris, Mason, Derek, Cameron, Brian. Our silly club means the world to me. Thank you for being solid friends. It's been crucial in keeping my head these past couple years.

My Moderators at The Crowded Table, Em, Mori, Beck, and Fern. Y'all are some of the most selfless humans I've ever met. You care so deeply and show me what it is to still be a human while interneting. I really don't tell you enough that I'm grateful for you.

Irreverent Media, Blake, Adrian, Janice, Josie, Roberto, Anna, Tori, Sarah, Justin, Brad, and the dozens of folks who help all of us behind the scenes, it's so cool to be creating a world where we can all find Joy again. I love y'all.

The Crowded Table Community, Thank you for supporting me with your words and your coins for YEARS now. I would never be able to do half of what I do without having y'all. I hope this blesses you in big ways.

And of course, you, sweet reader. I'll never be sick of hearing how this work has helped you. What a high compliment and affirmation of my vocation. Your support, you picking up this book, you sharing my work, it feels so delicious and I'm so thankful. There aren't enough words. If we're ever together in the same place, please say hello.

NOTES

READ THIS FIRST

4 *One way I heard Nadia Bolz-Weber*: Kevin Garcia, "#169: Anti-Excellence, w/ Nadia Bolz-Weber," May 2022, in *A Tiny Revolution*, podcast, https://open.spotify.com/episode/3GJaxKgSc3CtK9L8 1mxBqF?si=3be4e9fce7994d4c.

13 *A miracle is a shift in perception*: Dr. Helen Schucman, *A Course in Miracles: Combined Volume*, 3rd ed. (Mill Valley, CA: Foundation for Inner Peace, 2007).

CHAPTER 1

27 *Thích Nhất Hạnh, one of our most outstanding*: Thích Nhất Hạnh, *Body and Mind Are One: A Training in Mindfulness* (Boulder, CO: Sounds True, 2012).

31 *Abraham Hicks says that a belief*: Esther Hicks and Jerry Hicks, *The Vortex* (Carlsbad, CA: Hay House, 2019).

CHAPTER 2

51 *There has been a DreamSpace theft*: Tricia Hersey, *Rest Is Resistance* (New York: Little, Brown, 2022), 97–98.

56 *Rest is a meticulous love practice*: Hersey, *Rest Is Resistance*, 8.

57 *The last line of the first lesson*: Schucman, *A Course in Miracles*, W-1.4:3, https://acim.org/acim/lesson-1/nothing-i-see-means-anything/en/s/403#4:3.

61 *Committing to rest is a commitment to*: Heresy, *Rest Is Resistance*, 149.

64 *You only have to let the soft animal*: Mary Oliver, "Wild Geese," Poetry.com, https://www.poetry.com/poem/123017/wild-geese.

CHAPTER 3

71 *A Course in Miracles tells us*: Schucman, *A Course in Miracles*, T-15. XI.4:1-3, https://acim.org/acim/en/s/200#4:1-3 | T-15. XI.4:1-3.

77 *Until you have that thirst*: Swami Vivekananda, *Complete Works of Swami Vivekananda* (Reading Time, 2019), Kindle, 476.

CHAPTER 4

88 *According to fascinating research*: Brandon Flanery, "Study: Why People Are Leaving Christianity," https://brandonflanery.com/2022/12/13/why-people-are-leaving-christianity/.

90 *Father Richard Rohr, a living mystic*: Richard Rohr, *A Spring within Us: A Book of Daily Meditations* (Albuquerque, NM: CAC Publishing, 2016), 199–121.

93 *It's knowing what the water quality is*: Kevin Garcia, "#33: Petty and/or Prophetic, w/ Alicia Crosby," July 2017, in *A Tiny Revolution*, podcast, https://open.spotify.com/episode/1sDcaYr3IuqYGNWMWVTQCu.

CHAPTER 5

106 *Usually, I employ a technique*: Brené Brown, *Rising Strong and the Stories We Make Up*, 2020, PDF, https://brenebrown.com/wp-content/uploads/2021/09/Integration-Ideas_Rising-Strong_092221-1.pdf.

107 *Dr. Christena Cleveland says*: Christena Cleveland, *God Is a Black Woman*, (New York: HarperCollins, 2022), 91.

110 *A Course in Miracles says in lesson 135*: Schucman, *A Course in Miracles*, W-135.7:1–3, https://acim.org/acim/en/s/540#7:1–3.

112 *The Yoga Sutras of Patanjali offer us*: Sri Swami Satchidananda, trans., *Yoga Sutras of Patanjali: Commentary on the Raja Yoga Sutras by Sri Swami Satchidananda*, Sutra 1.33.

CHAPTER 6

132 *I've heard Ram Dass tell this story*: Dass, *Becoming Nobody.*

CHAPTER 7

139 *I couldn't stop talking about her*: Tina Fey, *Mean Girls*, directed by Mark Waters (Hollywood, CA: Paramount Pictures, 2004).

140 *A prayer I borrow from*: Marianne Williamson, *A Return to Love* (New York: HarperCollins, 2009) Kindle Edition, 160.

142 *Forgiveness is the healing of the perception of separation*: Schucman, *A Course in Miracles*, T-3.V.9:1, https://acim.org/acim/chapter-3/beyond-perception/en/s/75?wid=toc.

148 *Abraham Hicks, a modern Wisdom teacher*: Esther Hicks and Jerry Hicks, *Ask and It Is Given: Learning to Manifest Your Desires* (Carlsbad, CA: Hay House, 2004).

CHAPTER 8

155 *Octavia Butler said through her main character*: Octavia E. Butler, *Parable of the Sower* (New York: Open Road Media, 2012) Kindle Edition, 3.

156 *Octavia says in a later Earthseed verse*: Butler, *Parable of the Sower*, 31.

164 *I must not fear*: Frank Herbert, *Dune* (New York: Ace Books, 1965).

165 *I was listening to an interview*: Pete Holmes, "Elizabeth Gilbert," October 7, 2015, in *You Made It Weird with Pete Holmes*, podcast, https://podcasts.apple.com/us/podcast/elizabeth-gilbert/id475878118?i=1000354289925.

168 *Ram Dass said in a talk*: Dass, *Becoming Nobody.*

170 *I read a story in Sri Satchidananda's commentary*: Satchidananda, *The Yoga Sutras of Patanjali*.

CHAPTER 9

177 *In its introduction*: Schucman, *A Course in Miracles*, T-in.1:7–8, https:// acim.org/acim/en/s/51#1:7–8.

181 *Audre Lorde's essay*: Audre Lorde, "Uses of the Erotic," in *Sister Outsider* (New York: Penguin Books, 2020), 54.

184 *Thích Nhất Hạnh said that*: Thích Nhất Hạnh, *The Art of Living* (New York: Harper One, 2017), 68.

CHAPTER 10

205 *Octavia Butler says in her writing*: Butler, *Parable of the Sower*, 214.